Competition Policies
for the Global Economy

EDWARD M. GRAHAM
J. DAVID RICHARDSON

Competition Policies for the Global Economy

INSTITUTE FOR INTERNATIONAL ECONOMICS
Washington, DC
November 1997

Edward M. Graham, *Senior Fellow*, was Associate Professor in the Fuqua School of Business at Duke University (1988-90), Associate Professor at the University of North Carolina (1983-88); Principal Administrator of the Planning and Evaluation Unit at the OECD (1981-82); International Economist in the Office of International Investment Affairs at the US Treasury (1979-80) and Assistant Professor at the Massachusetts Institute of Technology (1974-78). He is author or coauthor of a number of studies of international investment and technology transfer, including *Global Corporations and National Governments* (1996) and *Foreign Direct Investment in the United States* (third edition 1995).

J. David Richardson, *Visiting Fellow*, is Professor of Economics in the Maxwell School of Citizenship and Public Affairs at Syracuse University and has written extensively on trade and international economic policy issues, including *Why Exports Really Matter* (1995), *Why Exports Matter More* (1996), *Sizing Up U.S. Export Disincentives* (1993), *International Economic Transactions: Issues in Measurement and Empirical Research* (1991), and *Issues in the Uruguay Round* (1988).

INSTITUTE FOR INTERNATIONAL ECONOMICS
11 Dupont Circle, NW
Washington, DC 20036-1207
(202) 328-9000   FAX: (202) 328-5432
http://www.iie.com

C. Fred Bergsten, *Director*
Christine F. Lowry, *Director of Publications*

Typesetting by Sandra F. Watts
Printing by Kirby Lithographic

Printed in the United States of America
99 98 97   5 4 3 2 1

Library of Congress Cataloging-in-Publication Data

Graham, Edward M. (Edward Montgomery), 1944–
    Competition Policies for the Global Economy
    Edward M. Graham and J. David Richardson.
        p. cm.—(Policy analyses in international economics; 51)
        Includes bibliographical references (p.).

    1. Competition, International.   2. Commercial policy.   3. International economic relations.   I. Richardson, J. David. II. Title.   III. Series.
    HF1414.G73   1997
    382'.3—dc21   97-26631
                                                             CIP

ISBN 0-88132-249-0

Contents

Preface

In recent years, a number of high-profile "international trade disputes" have involved private business practices that allegedly act as barriers to market access. In particular, controversy over these practices has been at the heart of United States-Japan disputes, including those over semiconductors, auto parts, and photographic film. Even more recently, the United States and the European Union narrowly averted a major clash over their sharply differing reactions to the merger of Boeing and McDonnell Douglas. More such disputes, involving many more nations and occurring especially in sectors that have traditionally been state-controlled but are now privatized, are quite likely.

Government regulation of private business practices falls within the realm of competition (or antitrust) policy. World trade law, as administered through the World Trade Organization (WTO), is not yet well equipped to handle such practices. Nonetheless, trade disputes centered on such issues are being taken to the WTO, and more such cases are coming. New international agreements are therefore needed to deal with these issues. In 1996, the WTO established a working group to examine the topic. Establishing new rules will not be easy, however, nor are all key WTO members even prepared to try. There are major substantive and procedural differences on the issue among the key nations and no clear consensus on what constitutes "best practice."

Indeed, economic analysis of many common private business practices that might impede market entry often shows they have hidden efficiencies, so there is no clear intellectual consensus on how to proceed. This is also an area where nations have been especially reluctant to cede authority to an international body. This book attempts to address these conceptual and policy problems. The authors first assess the intellectual basis for regulation of competition, concluding that the main goals of competition policy are to achieve fairness and efficiency. The best means of doing so are for governments to ensure that markets are as contestable as possible, that is that new entry by domestic and foreign firms be made as easy as possible. At the international level, governments might agree on certain initial steps to accomplish greater contestability: "national treatment" for foreign-controlled firms, abolition of most international cartels (including those that are now sanctioned), and establishment of mandatory consultation procedures when one government believes that private business practices in another nation foreclose exports or direct investment. There should also be premerger notification requirements for transborder or other mergers having cross-border effects. Further steps might be implemented at a future time.

The Institute for International Economics is a private nonprofit institution for the study and discussion of international economic policy. Its purpose is to analyze important issues in that area and to develop and communicate practical new approaches for dealing with them. The Institute is completely nonpartisan. The Institute is funded largely by philanthropic foundations. Major institutional grants are now being received from The German Marshall Fund of the United States, which created the Institute with a generous commitment of funds in 1981, and from The Ford Foundation, The Andrew W. Mellon Foundation, and The Starr Foundation. A number of other foundations and private corporations also contribute to the highly diversified financial resources of the Institute. Funding for this project was provided by the American Express Company and the Japan-United States Friendship Commission. About 12 percent of the Institute's resources in our latest fiscal year were provided by contributors outside the United States, including about 6 percent from Japan.

The Board of Directors bears overall responsibility for the Institute and gives general guidance and approval to its research program—including identification of topics that are likely to become important to international economic policymakers over the medium run (generally, one to three years), and which thus should be addressed by the Institute. The Director, working closely with the staff and outside Advisory Committee, is responsible for the development of particular projects and makes the final decision to publish an individual study. The Institute hopes that its studies and other activities will contribute to building a stronger foundation for international economic policy around the world. We invite readers of these publications to let us know how they think we can best accomplish this objective.

C. Fred Bergsten
Director
October 1997

1

Overview

Today's generation, far more than its predecessors, recognizes and pursues the rewards of highly competitive, global markets. Worldwide support for more open-market economic activity is still strong. However, there is resistance. Some is ideological, but much is structural. Structural resistance includes remaining border barriers to fully global market integration, such as tariffs, and entry (or behind-the-border) barriers to fully competitive markets, such as restrictions on the number of suppliers of banking, insurance, transportation, and telecommunications services.

What are the most important remaining barriers to open markets? No one has a persuasive answer. But most agree that border barriers are waning in importance relative to entry barriers. More precisely, tariffs, quotas, and border discrimination are being negotiated away, while regulatory and other barriers that protect incumbent firms by keeping out new suppliers are declining more slowly, especially in large services sectors. Sometimes even privatization replaces a public monopoly with a private monopoly. Consequently, many would agree that, over the past several decades, international trade has liberalized faster than domestic markets have.

This book tries to answer the questions that follow from these observations: If more open global markets are still desired, what is the most promising route? Is that route freer trade, freer entry, or some artful combination of the two? What provides the greatest resistance to open global markets? Is it public border barriers, private anticompetitive practices, proincumbent regulation, or some mix of these? What are the most feasible and attractive ways to enhance market access worldwide (what we will call contestability). Is it access for exporters, foreign investors, and new domestic suppliers alike, or is there already too much contest-ability? If there is too much, in what sense and under what circum-stances does this occur? Finally, what policies support contestability, both within and among countries?

The answers lie in judicious experimentation with a blend of prin-ciples, policies, and institutions. The ingredients come from the worlds of competition policy and international trade policy.

This study flows from fundamentals. However, to avoid boring the specialist, our account puts the fundamentals in new light and new con-text. In chapter 2, we describe the raison d'être of competition policy: how it interacts with trade policy, and why that interaction has become an international concern. Efficiency, fairness, and conflict are the key features.

In chapter 3, we outline policy initiatives that are both desirable and feasible in light of the fundamentals. First, we propose sensible first steps toward international cooperation that include fact-finding, consultation, dispute settlement, and maintenance of sovereign initiative. Then we propose a tougher but more rewarding second step: an agreement on Trade-Related Antitrust Measures (TRAMs) patterned on the Uruguay Round's Trade-Related Intellectual Property (TRIPS) agreement. The agree-ment would cover cartels, market-access-foreclosing practices, and merg-ers and acquisitions that are international in scope. Finally, we explore the long-run potential for replacing anticompetitive aspects of current trade

Box 2 Behind-the-border practices and international trade disputes

A number of recent international trade disputes have centered on barriers to market access that are behind-the-border in nature and fall into the domain of competition policy. One such case was the 1995 dispute between the governments of the United States and Japan over auto parts.

The issues raised in this dispute had little or nothing to do with border measures. Rather, the main issue was the level at which Japanese automakers (and firms engaging in servicing automobiles in Japan) purchased parts used as inputs to the production process from nontraditional suppliers. The United States Trade Representative (USTR) alleged that the Japanese auto makers relied for most purchases of parts on traditional Japanese suppliers with whom they have long-standing business relations. Foreclosure allegedly resulted, causing US auto parts manufacturers to lose potential sales even though (it was argued that) the US-made product was either better or lower in cost (or both) when compared to the Japanese-made product. It was further alleged that the same exclusive dealing was practiced by the US subsidiaries of Japanese automakers—that is, the Japanese firms Toyota, Nissan, and Honda also sourced most of their parts from only their traditional suppliers (including US subsidiaries of these suppliers).

It is not our intent here to evaluate the allegations or the remedial actions that were announced in June 1995 as part of a negotiated bilateral settlement of the dispute. We simply note that this was not a traditional trade policy dispute. Instead, it centers around basic issues of competition policy: the alleged exclusive dealing by the Japanese firms—a restrictive business practice that is considered a vertical restraint.

This is not the only such case in recent times that has raised issues of market foreclosure by virtue of vertical restraints. Earlier trade disputes between the United States and Japan over semiconductors raised many of the same issues as in the auto parts case, with the key difference that the vertical relationships in this instance were often intrafirm, that is, Japanese users of semiconductors often sourced these items from different divisions of the same company.

A recent US complaint against Japan involves control of distribution channels by Japan's major producer of photographic film and paper products, with the effect of allegedly foreclosing US exports. This case is currently before the WTO disputes settlement body.

remedies (antidumping and countervailing duties) with more efficient and more equitable competition-policy safeguards.

Competition policy and international trade policy are already being blended in the World Trade Organization (WTO) via two routes. First, a formal working group on trade and competition policy has been established to examine many of the same issues this book raises (see box 1). Second, certain recent international trade disputes before the WTO spring from issues of competition policy (see box 2).

2

The Philosophy and Economics
of Competition Policies in Open Economies

Concern with competition policy in global trade negotiations has mushroomed.[1] It is at the root of negotiations in airlines, basic telecommunications, financial services, insurance, and intellectual property. In these areas, international differences in regulatory regimes and rules have created highly varied competitive structures. As noted earlier, differences in generic competition policies have been central to recent trade disputes over market access for autos and auto parts and, more recently, for film and photographic products (see box 2). Such differences have also led to conflict over the announced merger of the US aerospace firms Boeing and McDonnell Douglas, which we address later.

Most of what has been written on competition policy is by and for specialists. By contrast, we make the case for a worldwide approach to competition policy based on economic principles. We then outline a

---

1. Scherer (1994) and Green and Rosenthal (1996) compare competition-policy regimes over time and in multiple countries and make policy recommendations. This study's companion volume, *Global Competition Policy* (Graham and Richardson 1997), covers these topics but emphasizes the fundamental economics and institutions as well as the integration of existing competition-policy and trade-policy structures at the global level. Scherer (1994) and Levinsohn (1996) are excellent introductions to the economics of competition policies in a global economy. Kühn, Seabright, and Smith (1992) and Ordover (1990) are equally good introductions to the economics of competition policy, but they pay less attention to the global economy. First, Fox, and Pitofsky (1991); Gifford and Matsushita (1996); and Mathewson, Trebilcock, and Walker (1990) are excellent introductions to legal aspects. Hindley (1996), Hoekman (1997a), Hoekman and Mavroidis (1994), and Lloyd and Sampson (1995) are good political and diplomatic introductions. See Graham (1994, 1995, 1996a, 1996b), Graham and Lawrence (1996), and Richardson (1995, 1997) for our contributions to this literature.

judicious agenda for action, ideally to inform the progress of the WTO's new working party.

Market Competition and Competition Policy: An Introduction

In the broadest sense, competition policy determines the institutional mix of competition and cooperation that gives rise to the market system. While competition is familiar to most, few reflect deeply on cooperation. Almost all market competitors are firms—business organizations (social groupings) that are, for the most part, internally cooperative, not competitive. Firms are the principal suppliers and buyers of most products and services, while consumers (households) generally buy only final goods, which are assembled from materials and components bought and sold many times by firms through a long series of exchanges in input markets and intrafirm transactions. The economic man or woman so common in elementary economics textbooks is a stylized fiction and so is the individual entrepreneur. Typical market transactions involve competition among firms. Many of these firms, including subtypes such as labor unions, can legally own and exchange property and differentiate and isolate their legal liability as a group from the liability of their members.

Thus, the market system is socially populated, socially rooted, socially conditioned, and socially constructed. It is far from the chaotically competitive law of the jungle that it is sometimes confused with. A global market system will be socially constructed and conditioned, too, by both policy design and cultural inertia.

This competitive-cooperative market system is governed by formal social regulations called competition policy. Competition policy aims to make the market work better. If designed properly, it is a market-perfecting part of the social infrastructure. It regulates the intensity of competition and the scope of cooperation and defines the legal boundaries for both. Examples of impermissible competition and impermissible cooperation, respectively, are predation (equivalent to the premeditated murder of a market competitor) and coercive collusion (one firm being forced to join a group of others).

Like all social regulations, competition policy reflects history and culture. Therefore, they are constantly changing, and they always differ among countries. Not all countries have a formal, codified competition policy,[2] but all have informal competition conventions. As markets be-

---

2. The number of countries implementing formal competition policies in recent years has risen sharply (Green and Rosenthal 1996; Tineo 1997). Most Eastern European and Latin American countries and South Korea, Mexico, and Taiwan have recently promulgated or revised their legislation. A number of other countries are in planning or drafting stages.

come global, however, differing competition policies and conventions have come into contact. Some of this contact has led to conflict, for example, over market access in China; some has led to constructive comparison, with an eye to identifying the fittest policies for growing global markets, as in deciding the type and duration of protection that an innovator needs from rivals who would copy his or her intellectual property.

To meet the two broad objectives of competition policies, efficiency and fairness, every country has developed conventions or rules of conduct for firms acting alone and together, over short intervals of time, and over their entire corporate lifetime. Below, we group these conventions into four concerns of competition policy. It turns out, unsurprisingly, that what is welcome competition policy from the perspective of one firm, one industry, or one country is not always welcome in other firms, industries, or countries. In many places, but especially in the last section of this chapter, we describe the ways that competition-policy objectives and concerns differ for an economy as a whole and for multiple economies in global interaction.

Objectives of Competition Policy: Efficiency and Fairness

Surprisingly, competition is not the objective of competition policy! Efficiency and fairness are the objectives, and when these conflict, the objective is to evaluate the tradeoff between them.

Goals and Instruments

Competition policies around the world seek a blend of efficiency and fairness[3] in their markets. Efficiency has a fairly clear economic meaning. It is a conservational objective; it aims to minimize waste. Efficiency is the ideal of getting the most out of the resources at hand. Examples are an efficient market that generates goods that buyers really want at least cost and an efficient charity that moves resources from one project to another so that the value of the good generated by those resources is at its highest. Likewise, an efficient society seeks the highest standard of living (material and nonmaterial) consistent with its available resources.

If society includes only those people currently living, and the relevant

---

3. Some countries de-emphasize fairness as an explicit goal of competition policy (e.g., the United States today). Others give it more prominence (e.g., the United Kingdom and France), as seen in Hay (1997) and Jenny (1997). Virtually all countries, however, include fairness considerations implicitly in implementing their competition policies. Neven, Nuttall, and Seabright (1993, 11) remark that an effective competition authority "must assist in the enfranchisement in the economic process of many of the interests that are naturally underrepresented in the alliance of managers and politicians that makes up the modern corporatist state. Shareholders, consumers, and potential employees. . . . an effective competition authority is the ally of all these excluded groups. . . ."

time frame is short (days, months, or even a few years), then that society pursues static efficiency. But if it includes future generations, and the relevant time frame is longer (five years, a decade, a new generation), it pursues dynamic efficiency. Practices that are statically efficient may not be dynamically efficient; the converse is also true. Thus, the simultaneous pursuit of dynamic and static efficiency involves tradeoffs.

The meaning of fairness, by contrast, is internationally nuanced and culturally distinctive. In the United States, it often means equality of opportunity or (in our context) free entry into a business endeavor. In other countries, it sometimes means that favored activity or loyalty should be rewarded, or that equity of process or outcome (market division according to historic shares) is valued. Years of acrimonious bilateral negotiations have revealed that Japanese auto and consumer electronics firms characterize loyalty toward and from their traditional suppliers as "only fair," while potential US rivals find it to be an unfair foreclosing of their market access.

Indeed, emphasizing fairness almost invites contention, acrimony, and even international conflict when the protagonists are of different nationalities. But there is no denying the importance of fairness as a motive for competition policy; hence, there is a clear need for definition of what is and what is not fair in a market system and for mutual recognition of threshold standards of fairness in international competition. This need is great because the concepts of fairness and, especially, fair trade have been much abused by special interest groups.

Competition can be a means to attaining efficiency and fairness. For example, a perfectly competitive market—in which there are many small firms that freely enter and exit an industry that produces a standardized product—often achieves efficiency and equality of opportunity (fairness). But this is not always the case. In the market for innovation, perfect competition is generally believed to deliver (inefficiently) too little (see below).[4] For a natural monopoly, a single supplier for the entire market is efficient—competition is not. Where buyers of a product have varied needs and specifications, such that efficiency requires a multitude of varieties rather than one standardized product, monopolistic competition—where numerous producers of those varieties have limited monopoly power and can enter and exit freely—is efficient. And perfect competition makes no promise about fairness of process or outcome, only fairness of opportunity.

Efficiency and fairness are the prizes for competition policy; competition is a secondary objective or, more accurately, an instrument.[5] It

---

4. See also Scherer (1992, 22-40) and Scherer and Ross (1990, chapter 17).

5. Countries differ to the extent that this is true. The United States has sometimes made having many small competitors the chief goal of competition policies, as in the days of trust-busting. Japan, by contrast, explicitly worries about excessive competition (see Suzumura 1997).

will, however, be convenient to use the term anticompetitive (somewhat like the term antisocial) to describe practices and structures that interfere with the objectives of efficiency or fairness. Rule of reason is a corollary legal concept that is relevant to many cases where considerations of fairness or efficiency (and tradeoffs between these) require subtle judgments and balancing of arguments. Under rule of reason, these judgments are made on the basis of circumstances and probable outcome rather than fixed per se rules.

Efficiency-Fairness Tradeoffs and Cross-Country Conflicts

Efficiency and fairness, like oil and water, do not mix easily. Under most circumstances, neither objective can be met without some sacrifice on the other. Conflict between these objectives occurs within countries and among them.

Within countries, conflict occurs when business practices that enhance the efficiency of some firms appear unfair to others, or when policies that treat all situations fairly have a high efficiency cost. Mergers between firms (e.g., between two large telecommunications companies) often involve efficiency for insiders at the apparent cost of fairness to outsiders. Grants of exclusive property rights to patented innovations and unique industrial processes involve the same tradeoff.

Nonetheless, apparently evenhanded bans on all forms of collusion can force fairness at the cost of efficiency. For some purposes, such as product standard setting, cooperation among firms (collusion to a cynic) can reduce resources expended on the promotion of competing standards (the early competition between VHS and Beta formats for videotapes may be an example of such inefficient expenditures). Global cooperation among firms and governments, as occurs in Mutual Recognition Agreements (MRAs) over the standards each country sets for various products, can also reduce waste.

Cross-country conflicts in competition policies are increasing, because concepts of fairness often differ. Some of these differences are endemic (cultural); some are generic. Examples of endemic differences are US insistence on due legal process and continental European and Asian preferences for administrative process (see Fox 1997a; Jenny 1997; Kühn 1997; Matsushita 1997; Vernon and Nicolaïdis 1997). Examples of generic differences are the way fairness is seen by would-be entrants and by incumbents, by firms that are small and large, by single-product and diversified firms, and by privately owned, publicly owned, and state-owned firms. Differences in perceived fairness also arise because firm ownership differs from country to country. France and China, for example, have far more state-owned firms than do the United Kingdom, Germany, or the United States. French and Chinese entry barriers in sectors dominated by such firms are contentious to would-be rivals. The

United States requires scrupulous financial reporting because most large firms' equities are widely held in public stock markets, but such reporting seems burdensome and unfair to firms that are partly family-owned (as in Taiwan) or corporately owned through a tight network of cross-firm shareholdings (as in Japan).

Sometimes, efficiency issues also cause international conflict over competition policies. For example, some countries seek static efficiency and others seek dynamic efficiency. Countries that pursue the former may more strictly regulate cooperative high-technology activities than do those that pursue the latter.[6] Countries that pursue dynamic efficiency may subsidize innovation but force innovating companies to license imitators at a regulated price ceiling. These differences cause conflict between firms that compete with each other on seemingly uneven playing fields; such conflict occurred between US and Japanese firms in the early 1980s prior to changes in US competition policy that loosened restrictions on research and development consortiums.

An even more important example is that what's efficient for one country isn't always efficient for the world. Export cartels and monopoly marketing boards are prime examples. Every country can by itself achieve national efficiency—the most output from its national resources—by ensuring perfect competition in the domestic market while charging foreign buyers a monopolistic price in export sales. The country's residents then earn monopoly rents from foreign buyers but do not pay any efficiency cost.[7] However, if every country followed this practice, collective inefficiencies in world export sales world loom large. Such differing effects on national efficiency were well illustrated in the treatment of the proposed merger of Boeing and McDonnell Douglas. European competition-policy authorities initially concluded that the merger might be anticompetitive for Europe, whereas US competition-policy authorities found that it was efficient for the United States. The conflict

---

6. See, for example, Katz and Ordover (1990). Many chapters in Jorde and Teece (1992) argue that US competition policies are insufficiently future oriented for either long-run US welfare (i.e., future gains are inefficiently foregone) or for the ideal US position in the global economy. But competition among firms to arrive at the ideal type and timing of innovations is on balance favorable, and strong competition policies that insure entry by energetic new firms often best deliver dynamic efficiency. For a detailed review of the evidence on how market structure affects dynamic efficiency, see Scherer and Ross (1990, chapter 17).

7. Or, to be maximally efficient, a country by itself could offer foreign sellers a monopsonistic price on imports it buys. That is essentially what the economists' famous optimal tariff does. It beats down world supply prices of imports to the level that a sole national buyer would offer and collects rent (monopsonistic surplus) from the world's sellers of those imports. Alternatively, in a few cases, a government essentially makes itself the sole buyer of imports on behalf of its own constituents, as in certain import-licensing schemes.

was resolved with a compromise that somewhat reduced potential efficiency in the United States (e.g., by undoing exclusive-selling agreements between Boeing and certain US airlines that might have led to cost reductions in aircraft maintenance) while reducing what was perceived in Europe as anticompetitive behavior (e.g., undoing the exclusive-selling agreements increased market access for Boeing's European rival, Airbus Industrie).

Finally, and fundamentally, conflict among nations exists for one simple, yet easy-to-forget reason: no firm prefers competition in its output market. However successfully competition may deliver efficiency and fairness to a market system as a whole (sellers, buyers, and final consumers), each firm would rather have less competition as a seller:[8] a monopoly would be most preferred. This is true of market-leading firms and for those hanging on for survival. It is also true for global competition. So skepticism is appropriate when one firm complains about the anticompetitive behavior of a rival (each would do the same if it could get away with it), and also when one country's firms complain collectively about the unfair, anticompetitive behavior of foreign rivals. But skeptic should not be surprised at the complaint, nor, for that matter, be unsympathetic. Global competition policy is an issue precisely because some of these complaints are well taken.

The Efficiency Objective

In almost every country, competition policy aims to reduce inefficiencies. One of the most familiar inefficiencies is the wasteful underproduction and overpricing of a monopolist with market power. Almost as familiar are distortions in relative prices and costs that mislead investors and buyers. Less familiar inefficiencies are excessive product standardization or its opposite: wasteful product differentiation, unduly sluggish innovation or unnecessary duplication of research effort, inadequate realization of scale economies, and underprovisioning of future generations.

The Fairness Objective

There is also a distributional economics of competition policy, concerned with process and fairness in markets. Its most obvious expression is in policies that oppose coercion and various abuses of market power that imply involuntary action. When economists defend the market system, they require volunteerism. That is, they rule out coercion (no reputable economist recommends markets for slavery, contract murder, or mercenaries to fight wars of territorial aggression). Many competition policies

---

8. As buyers of inputs, of course, firms prefer input-market competition, including that created by free opportunities to import and outsource inputs.

are the legislative expression of the anticoercion principle.[9] Other policies prohibit abuses of market power, such as a horizontal cartel's boycott of distributors that deal with outsiders or new suppliers. Several years ago, Japanese producers of flat glass were found to practice such abuses, and similar issues are at the heart of the ongoing Japan-US dispute in the WTO over alleged abuses in the markets for film and other photographic supplies (see box 2).

Other process-oriented competition policies include those that outlaw fraud, criminalize the theft of intellectual property and industrial secrets, discipline predation, regulate price discrimination (charging different prices to different buyers), and ban foreclosure (contracts and other arrangements with suppliers or distributors that completely exclude new firms). For example, the European Union recently accused Boeing of negotiating 20-year exclusive-supplier contracts with American Airlines, Continental Airlines, and Delta Air Lines, though some reports suggest that Europe's Airbus had equal chances to compete for and win those and any other contracts.[10]

The efficiency and fairness objectives of competition policy are discussed at several levels. The most familiar is in the context of a single market for one product. We start there in the next section, and then move to the less familiar competition-policy concerns of an economy in which many products and services are sold. We conclude this discussion with a treatment of multiple economies in international contact.

Sectoral Concerns of Competition Policy

Competition policy at the sectoral level aims for an efficient and fair market to ensure that short-term decisions such as pricing and long-term decisions such as investments for innovation are made efficiently and fairly by firms, whether acting alone or with other firms. It also weighs a sector's efficiency and fairness rules against other social objectives, such as the defense industry's role in national security. In subsections below, we describe the four concerns of competition policy as firm behavior, relational behavior, lifetime behavior, and social behavior.

However, competition policy cannot be so easily apportioned. Each subsection describes policy concerns that are linked organically to the other subsections. For example, predation is the premeditated goal of a

---

9. From this point of view, for example, laws against employment of underage (child) workers is a species of competition policy.

10. See, for example, Laura D'Andrea Tyson, "McBoeing" Should Be Cleared for Takeoff, *Wall Street Journal*, 22 July 1997, A14.

single firm, but the concept obviously involves a victim firm and is perversely relational.[11]

Firm Behavior

Competition policy is first of all concerned with a firm's behavior and market power. At any moment,[12] this concern involves inefficiencies in prices or marketing, inequities in the treatment of customers or potential rivals, and other abuses of market power. These concerns, sometimes called restrictive business practices, implicitly involve assessments of how close a firm's prices come to its costs; how closely a firm meets buyer demand for products of varying size, durability, reliability, and other characteristics; and how freely a firm will allow rival firms and products to emerge. Competition-policy authorities never try to comprehensively or continuously monitor corporate decision making on these details, much less to direct it. But when anticompetitive behavior is suspected, most authorities have the legal right to summon detailed information from firms in their jurisdiction.[13]

In brief, the first concern of competition policy is to discipline the market power of firms. But what exactly is market power? And what are its inefficiencies and abuses?

Price Setting

Market power is first defined with reference to price and then with respect to attributes. Firms that have the capacity to choose their own price from a menu of options, ranging from high prices with low sales to low prices with high sales, are said to have price-setting power. Firms that can produce any mix of product varieties (e.g., high or low quality, durability, and flexibility) are said to have attribute-selection power.[14]

---

11. The technical distinction between the sections called "Firm Behavior" and "Relational Behavior" is that the first involves a firm's noncooperative (i.e., independent) behavior, while the second involves its cooperative (i.e., joint) behavior with some other firm(s).

12. We consider the lifetime behavior of a firm below.

13. The problem of gathering such detailed information is reduced in countries such as the United States, which allow firms, presumably well-informed, to initiate competition-policy legal action against rivals that they accuse of anticompetitive behavior. The US rewards for successful legal action can be three times as large as the damages (treble damages).

14. Other descriptions refer to a firm's power to select optimal characteristics, differentiation, niche, quality, position, location, performance, and model. Competition over product attributes is sometimes called (blandly) nonprice competition. Besanko, Dranove, and Shanley (1996, part III) describe it as competition for "strategic positioning." Katz and Ordover (1990) and Jorde and Teece (1992) make much of the need for competition policy to ensure the efficiency of competition in innovation, in addition to the more familiar (static) price competition.

In reality, most firms have some degree of price-setting and attribute-selection power. But both kinds of power are limited by the prices and attributes that rival firms choose. In the perfectly competitive extreme, power is perfectly limited to a single price ceiling and a single attribute floor (e.g., a wheat farmer sells nothing if the price he asks exceeds any rival's price that day or if the cleanliness and purity of the wheat falls short of the minimal acceptable standard of the least discriminating buyer). In a market structure called monopolistic competition, a firm has price-setting power over the precise blend of attributes that makes its product unique. But other firms produce so many close substitutes to that attribute package that the firm's price choices range over a narrow band, and its power can be severely constrained.[15] At the other extreme, monopoly, both price-setting power and attribute-selection power are maximal, because such a firm is the sole producer of a product with no close substitutes. The term oligopoly describes a market structure in which a small number of firms produce a product with no close substitutes; as the number of rivals and substitutes increases, oligopoly bleeds into monopolistic competition.

Price-setting market power usually leads a firm to boost profits by supplying less to buyers than would be socially ideal but also charging a higher price than is ideal (there is, however, one important exception—see "Price Discrimination" below).[16] That is, of course, fine with the firm's shareholders, but the social ideal is for a firm to keep on selling as long as buyers are willing to pay enough for each successive unit to cover the extra cost of producing that unit.[17] If the firm stops short of this ideal, there is inefficiency (waste) and unwelcome frustration—some buyers are rationed (unfairly, they would claim) and fail to receive units of a product that cost less to produce than their own valuation of those units. That firms will behave this way is at the core of both microeconomic theory and the efficiency objective of competition policy.[18]

---

15. The technical condition is that every firm's cross-price elasticity of demand with respect to substitute products is very high and increases with the number of substitutes. In that event, its own price elasticity will necessarily be very high as well, as described in the appendix. When attributes involve many dimensions, however (e.g., quality, location, and durability), an increased number of rivals along any given dimension can sometimes work in the opposite direction, enhancing price-setting and other market power.

16. Microeconomic reasoning shows that, for modest sales reductions, starting at the ideal price and quantity, a firm's overall revenues decline more slowly than its overall costs, generating extra profit, which can often be identified with excess (or supernormal or economic) profit.

17. The technical name for this is the socially optimal price and quantity. See the appendix for an alternative description.

18. These materials are introduced in a slightly more technical way in the appendix, as is the following material.

Price Discrimination

There is one important exception to these generalizations about price setting. When a firm's price-setting power is enhanced by price-discriminating power, wasteful inefficiency (rationing) can be reduced, although fairness concerns become sharper. Price discrimination is the power of a firm to charge different prices to different groups of customers (who find it impossible or uneconomical to resell the firm's goods among themselves).[19] Examples of price discrimination are time-of-day pricing for telephone calls and power use, loyalty discounts to recurrent customers, and differing fares for the same airline flight for leisure travelers and business travelers. In the extreme, a perfect price discriminator has the power to charge each customer a unique price—all that each customer can bear to own the product rather than to do without. Thus, whatever its effect on efficiency, price discrimination accentuates overpricing and makes it discriminatory as well. Both effects raise fairness concerns.

Price-setting power enhanced by this extreme form of price discrimination can restore the ideal volume of sales (and eliminate inefficiency). The firm keeps selling until it reaches the least-willing customer, who values the product so little that he or she bids barely enough to cover the extra cost of the last few units that the firm produces. That is, by definition, the social ideal. But with price-discriminating power, the firm is able to overprice by more, and its profits are higher, because it is able to extract every last dollar of customer benefit[20] above the minimum necessary[21] to keep its customers buying at all!

More common (and less extreme) price-discriminating power may create new inefficiency, rather than relieving it, however. Currency fluctuations within the European Union, for example, contribute to European firms' power to isolate national markets from each other and charge different prices to different national buyers despite the absence of trade barriers. One of the motives for European Monetary Union is to reduce this type of price discrimination, which inefficiently deters trade between arbitraging buyers in low-price/low-value countries—buyers who become secondary-market sellers to buyers in high-price/high-value countries.[22] Even under a currency union, however, national regulations on which and how many firms can be authorized sellers may continue to support

---

19. Customers who would be charged high prices would otherwise stop buying directly from the firm and start buying indirectly from customers who could get the product at lower prices; these less desperate customers would begin to buy not only for themselves, but also to resell (arbitrage) merchandise to the first group.

20. Technically, the customer's consumer surplus.

21. Technically, the customer's reservation price; such discrimination is called first degree.

22. See, for a discussion, When the Walls Come Down, *The Economist*, 5 July 1997, 61-63.

this type of price discrimination. But such regulations are scrutinized strictly by the EU competition-policy authorities. Not only do such regulations support price discrimination, but they may also condemn the overall volume of European sales to be inefficiently lower than even a single-price monopoly would allow.

In any case, price-discriminating power almost always involves a significant and discriminatory transfer of purchasing power from buyers to extra profit for sellers,[23] and this may be considered unfair.[24] So price discrimination changes the nature of the competition-policy problem but not necessarily its intensity, probably putting more weight on unfairness than on inefficiency.[25]

The power to price discriminate is increasingly important. The technologies for identifying and isolating customer groups continue to advance (e.g., cash registers and websites that keep track of what, when, and how much a credit-card customer buys and match such information to socioeconomic characteristics from the customer's credit records). And the cost of frequently varying prices has been greatly reduced by computerized real-time price lists (e.g., airfares in reservations systems) and discounts keyed to coupons and bar codes. For competition policy, the interesting implication of rising price discrimination is a justifiable shift in attention toward ensuring fairness and a competitive process and away from efficiency concerns (which often take care of themselves, especially when entry to price-discriminating activities is unencumbered). Partly for these reasons, we organize our policy recommendations with a priority on competitive process. Our recommendations are aimed at making markets more internationally contestable—that is, making them open to entry by as many new competitors, foreign or domestic, as choose to compete.

Price discrimination has increasing prominence in international conflict as well. Past international trade conventions allow countries to protect against injurious imports priced lower in their country than in the source country. This form of price discrimination is labeled dumping, and the protective tariffs to combat it are called antidumping duties. To the extent that these duties reduce cross-border price discrimination, they may enhance fairness (indeed, dumping is one example of so-called

---

23. The extra profit may attract new entrants to the industry, thus shifting the market outcome toward efficient (ideal) outcomes (see Varian 1989, 619-22). Our focus on single-firm behavior allows us to ignore that issue here.

24. It is controversial whether there is a fairness problem at all. Price discrimination in innovation, for example, is considered by many analysts to be part of the reward to those who have pioneered. See, for example, Katz and Ordover (1990, 139).

25. It also changes the confidence economists have giving expert advice. They usually feel more secure discussing efficiency than the fairness of distributional outcomes between buyers and sellers.

unfair trade), but they almost surely inhibit efficiency. While all tariffs are price-distorting wedges between foreign and domestic suppliers, anti-dumping duties are aimed only at dumping suppliers and not all suppliers, making the distortion discriminatory (for a discussion of the tradeoffs involved, see Lipstein [1997]).

Attribute Competition

Attribute-selection power can sometimes, but not always, have unwelcome effects similar to those of price-setting power, involving both inefficiency and inequity. Powerful incumbent firms may offer too few models or models that are too old—and it may overprice them too.[26] For example, airline competition often underprovides desirable attributes. Every airline route serves both business and leisure passengers, whose ideal service requirements differ. Sometimes incumbent airlines will strategically choose (and price) flight times, aircraft, and service to make it unprofitable for a rival firm to generate attribute diversity—that is, to produce substitute models around the ones already in existence.[27] For example, an established business-oriented airline may offer frequent flights to nearby cities and modest (but not rock-bottom) prices to deter a leisure-oriented rival airline from competing. The number and type of service attributes offered by the established incumbent may still be less than ideal;[28] that is, some (leisure) buyers are rationed and, thus, are unable to buy a type of service (e.g., flights on weekends) that would actually cost less to produce than the buyer's valuation of that service. That is wasteful. It may also be an abuse of market power by the incumbent. Exclusionary behavior can undermine both efficiency (measured by the rationing cost) and fairness (because potential rivals are closed out).

This kind of strategic attribute selection may not always be anticompetitive: strategic entry deterrence is not always bad and not always unfair. The incumbent airline in the example does, after all, increase

---

26. Again, the statement implies a social ideal. When buyers differ from each other, their varying tastes for proximity, quality, durability, convenience, and so on will usually make it ideal for a sector to produce many models. But how many models in all? How many models for each firm? These are similar questions to "how much should a firm produce?" The answers, though, are unfamiliar and not clear-cut. See Besanko, Dranove, and Shanley (1996, part III) for the firm's answers, but see the discussion of lifetime behavior (below) for the conclusion that markets may not always generate the socially ideal attribute selection.

27. An analogous strategy in innovation is for the innovating firm to design a patent so that it blocks rivals from designing substitute patents around the innovator's patent. For obvious reasons, this is called a blocking patent.

28. But not enough less to grant an entrant any profit after it pays the fixed costs of set-up.

density and frequency and reduce price.[29] In doing so, it no doubt satisfies some leisure travelers. Thus, as is often the case, whether there is an abuse or inefficiency here is a judgment call.[30] That is one reason why competition policies worldwide appeal to a rule of reason in deciding whether practices such as entry deterrence involve exclusion or other distortions or inequities.

Best-Practice Competition

Market power can allow a firm to be nonchalant about maintaining the most efficient production techniques and, thereby, raise its costs. One way this happens is through sluggish innovation, discussed below. However, a firm with market power might also allow costs to rise wastefully unchecked by the discipline of having to keep them in line with costs of rival firms. Inadequate cost control often results in overstaffing and excessive salaries. Also, prices paid for buildings, machines, and intermediate products might be excessive (e.g., a headquarters building that is more a monument than an efficient office). Such bloat in organizations is often termed x-inefficiency.

Yet another source of inefficient inputs is costly efforts to deter rivals and maintain market power. These efforts can include lobbying of government agencies that brings benefits to the firm but is wasteful from society's perspective. To deter rivals, the firm might overbuild capacity or commit to making products with attributes that the firm cannot produce as efficiently as can potential rival firms.

Enhanced contestability in a market often leads firms to improve cost control and performance (see Scherer and Ross 1990, 667-78, for evidence on these effects). Likewise, enhanced contestability can lead to favorable restructuring of industries, allowing those firms that are adaptable and effective to absorb the business of those that are not and, thus, improving performance of the industry (see Tybout and Westbrook [1995] for evidence that these effects were important for Mexican industry following liberalization in the late 1980s).

Predation

In an extreme application of market power that is least favorable to efficiency and fairness, an established airline not only deters would-be rivals, but successfully preys upon new entrants. Such predation is the strategic, temporary deployment by the predator firm of attributes that are so attractive (and prices that are so low) that existing rivals leave a

---

29. This is compared to what they would do if entry were not a concern (e.g., if the government had granted them a legal monopoly on the routes).

30. Price discrimination also illustrates the need for judgment calls.

market, allowing the predator firm subsequently to enhance market power by reducing quality, raising price, and deterring reentry. Though such predation clearly would be anticompetitive, its real-life occurrence seems rare.[31] Ordinarily, it seems, a firm is only displaced by another firm that offers indefinitely lower prices, better quality, and higher performance. As a temporary tactic to gain market power and then abuse it, predation has proved unsuccessful.[32]

Contestability

However, there is an extreme case of only apparent market power that is favorable to efficiency and equity. An airline resolved to deter rivals or displace an incumbent might be forced (by the ease with which rivals can come and go) to offer so many flights at such low prices for so long a time that the outcome comes close to what would have occurred with realized entry by those rivals. This type of market is called perfectly contestable. In such a market, the varieties offered and their prices come close to the social ideal even when there are only a few firms selling.[33] In general, markets can be made more contestable (hence more efficient) if potential entrants can enter and exit freely and if set-up and withdrawal (exit) costs are low.[34]

From this perspective, global liberalization can be an important force for contestability by multiplying the number of potential entrants and reducing set-up and withdrawal costs. There are usually more potential entrants after trade and investment liberalization. When entering a market,

---

31. There are some cases of true price predation in the airline industry. For example, incumbent carriers on North Atlantic routes dropped their prices in response to new entry during the 1980s to drive the new entrants out of the market. However, such predation seems rare. In 95 percent of the US and EU antidumping cases they examined where predatory behavior could, in principle, have motivated the dumping, Shin (1992) and Bourgeois and Messerlin (1993) reject even the possibility of predation. The organization for Economic Cooperation and Development (OECD) (1989) has a comprehensive treatment of general predatory pricing, whether linked to dumping or not; it covers economic reasoning and historical precedents in all OECD countries.

32. Over the lifetime of firms, discussed below, this more common and procompetitive type of displacement is called creative destruction; Schumpeter (1950) gives its classic description.

33. Bresnahan and Reiss (1991) find, for example, in a study of regional markets for professional services, that markets come very close to the social ideal after the third, fourth, or fifth firm enters.

34. Technically, the set-up costs that matter are irrecoverably sunk. That means that they cannot be reclaimed in the event of withdrawal or transferred to some other use. Licensing and license fees are examples of set-up costs that policy has some influence over. Long-term contracts with municipal authorities (e.g., over taxes) and regulations covering the need to notify workers before layoffs are examples of withdrawal costs that policy has influence on.

established firms from abroad may have lower set-up costs than would completely new domestic entrants. Thus, liberalization that makes the potential entry of those established firms more likely enhances contestability. Liberalization affects set-up costs in several ways:

- Foreign firms may no longer need to pay for licenses to ship their goods as imports (of the domestic country).

- Foreign firms may no longer need to pay (or bribe) various middlemen (e.g., mandated joint-venture partners) to establish their investors on a par with local firms. Liberalization may alter withdrawal costs as well.

- Suppliers of exports to the domestic market will obviously not have to meet the same withdrawal requirements as a domestic firm that employs local labor and pays local taxes.[35]

In these and many other ways, globalization makes markets more contestable.[36]

Natural Monopoly

So-called natural monopoly represents still another extreme, however, in which technology dictates either scale economies or high natural set-up costs, and there is no natural limit on capacity for the relevant market. In this extreme, the average cost per unit for a firm is far lower at high-volume production than at low-volume, because the fixed set-up costs can be spread over many units of production, and capacity constraints never appear.[37] Therefore, it becomes efficient (cost saving) for a firm to operate at high volume. A natural monopoly exists when there are still cost savings from higher-volume production even at the point where a single firm serves an entire market. In this case, price-setting and attribute-selection market power may be the inevitable companions of technological efficiency. Competition policy then traditionally aims to minimize the inefficiencies and inequities that could result under natural monopoly. It may set a ceiling on the price charged by the natural

---

35. For example, notification and severance requirements, fulfillment of long-term leases, etc.

36. See Graham and Lawrence (1996), Feketekuty and Rogowsky (1996), and Hoekman (1997a) for further development of the presumption that global liberalization makes markets more contestable.

37. To be a valid natural monopoly, the set-up costs must also be sunk (see note 36). This makes natural monopoly rare, because many machines or factories can be sold to another sector or to users abroad—as is true of many machine tools and even whole refineries, breweries, and factories (see Andrew Taylor, Third World Goes Bargain Hunting, *Financial Times*, reprinted in *National Times*, June 96, 20). Set-up costs in these cases may be large, but they are not sunk.

monopolist;[38] it may force firms to rebid periodically on the license to be the natural monopolist; or it may deny the natural monopolist's preference to exclude specialized rivals from using its infrastructure or networks[39] or regulate the price it charges rivals to use them.

Globalization of markets and technological change have clearly reduced the importance of some natural monopolies. Satellites and other forms of wireless communication, for example, have removed the necessity to pay up-front for wire-dependent telecommunications networks.[40] The need for competition policy to deal with natural monopolies has been correspondingly reduced, as has the need for international competition-policy conventions in these cases.

However, globalization and technological change have created a new class of natural monopoly—the global natural monopoly, which has falling average costs for its products and services even if it serves the whole world. Putative examples are hypersonic and large commercial aircraft; high-technology weapons; and some banking, insurance, and satellite transmission services.[41] For these products, the case for competition policy may have been accentuated, and because the efficient monopoly exists at the global level, the corresponding competition-policy regime is international.[42] The recent merger of Boeing and McDonnell Douglas illustrates the potential for severe competition-policy inconsistency and conflict among subglobal policy authorities.

Size Is Not Power

Natural monopoly and perfect contestability have one trait in common, though they are different types of extreme market structure. They both show that big firms are not automatically bad for efficiency or fairness. "Small may be beautiful," as some say, but it may also be inefficient; to have multiple suppliers may seem fairer than to have only one, but it is not necessarily fairer if one firm has an edge over the others and can serve the entire market best.

---

38. For example, the US Federal Communications Commission sets a maximum price that local owners of wire-based telephone networks can charge long-distance companies for access to those networks.

39. Telecommunications rivals that provide value-added services beyond normal telephone service, such as access to data, are an example. See Graham and Lawrence (1996).

40. The difference between the cost of wire-dependent infrastructure and launch costs has allowed remote, previously unserved areas to have basic telecommunications.

41. For the banking and insurance sectors, the potential for global natural monopoly arises from the creation of electronic-payment clearing systems.

42. Yet the strength of the new case is controversial; each example faces close substitutes (e.g., subsonic aircraft, conventional weapons) that may so diminish the efficiency and fairness costs of the global natural monopoly that the problem is not worth worrying about. See the appendix.

By implication, antitrust-mandated breakups of large firms may sometimes be neither efficient nor fair, and, as much as these firms plague populists, visceral concerns over the awesome power of megamultinational firms may be sadly misplaced.[43]

It is not that the market automatically makes all well or that anticompetitive abuses are minimal. On the contrary—that is why competition policy is an issue within and between countries. The point is that the size of a firm is rarely a good indicator of its power. Even small firms can have market power in specialty segments of markets, and even they can abuse that power. And large firms often find their power surprisingly constrained by competition from others.

Furthermore, when big firms and sole suppliers have little market power, they also have close to average (normal) profits. They are not making extraordinary amounts of money for their owners, management, or host countries. Competition and trade policies that aim to preserve extraordinary profit pools for one's own domestic firms or to shift them away from foreign firms are less relevant to the extent that even big firms have small and fleeting market power. Many analysts feel that the growth of trade and the investment-based cross-penetration of national markets has produced the situation described above: global markets in which the typical structure is monopolistic competition, not oligopoly. The competition policies that correspond to such a world have many fewer sectoral exemptions, and the trade policies that correspond make less sense from a strategic standpoint.

Relational Behavior

Bad and Good

Competition policy is concerned with interfirm behavior as well as the behavior of each firm alone. This explicitly involves scrutinizing mergers and cooperative joint ventures and challenging those that are anticompetitive.[44] Formal cartels that bind firms together in what is essentially a monopoly are usually banned (with some exceptions), and the authorities watch carefully for less formal collusion that has the same effect.

---

43. Scherer (1994, 87-88) concludes that there is little theoretical or empirical support for the proposition that multinational firms (size notwithstanding) are different from "companies that have equivalent market positions but operate from only a single nation."

44. A merger legally blends the ownership and management of two companies. A joint venture (or strategic alliance) is a less formal form of cooperation, occasionally involving the creation of equity in an entirely new, joint, and dedicated unit but more typically involving no equity exchange or issue. Neven, Nuttall, and Seabright (1993) provide a detailed reference on supranational issues in merger policies for open economies, focusing on the European Union.

Relational concerns aim to make sure that firms do compete with each other, rather than merely fake it. No firm welcomes competition as a seller, as discussed above, so there is always a danger of implicit live-and-let-live collusion. Thus, firms can appear to compete while colluding to avoid aggressive actions such as price competition or while secretly dividing up attribute niches among themselves so that each is a mini-monopolist in reserved models or submarkets or while ostracizing or punishing uncooperative rivals that refuse to join in the collusion such as by denying them access to some vital input (e.g., a pipeline or communications network).

Anticompetitive mergers and collusive practices, such as price fixing and market-swapping quotas, involve the familiar inefficiencies and inequities. They waste resources, exclude a margin of buyers who would have been willing to pay the costs of more production or more variety, and suck purchasing power away from those buyers that remain.

But not all interfirm cooperation is anticompetitive collusion. A merger in which a strong firm takes over a weak one and restructures it to preserve at least some of its business and employment may enhance overall market efficiency and be fairer than allowing the weak firm to fail and close down. That was an essential part of Boeing's defense of its takeover of McDonnell Douglas's commercial aircraft business. A research joint venture in which each firm takes responsibility for developing and patenting different aspects of a new process or parts of a new product, but then makes licenses available to all members, may efficiently value the spillovers from one firm's innovation to other firms—spillovers that markets find notoriously hard to value.[45] A system in which a firm bans its retailers and distributors from selling any products except its own (e.g., if Fuji or Kodak insisted that developers and processors of film use only theirs) may enhance informational advertising and efficient quality maintenance—they give each distributor incentives and objectives similar to those of the manufacturer—though such practices may indeed appear otherwise to be anticompetitive barriers to entry. Finally, the incentive for and returns from innovation have been shown (e.g., Geroski 1992) to generally rise when firms are permitted to cooperate with suppliers of complementary inputs (e.g., Microsoft cooperating with both software developers and computer makers or Toyota cooperating with Nippondensu).

Horizontal and Vertical

There are two broad types of interfirm cooperation, horizontal and vertical. Horizontal cooperation involves similar firms at similar stages in

---

45. Such spillovers, called externalities, are a classic case of problems that markets do not solve well.

the production process (e.g., raw processor, assembler, or distributor); vertical cooperation involves complementary firms at different stages. Competition policy is more suspicious of horizontal cooperation than of vertical. Horizontal cooperation smells more like collusion, like cartels, and the burden of proof to the contrary is usually on the firms. Vertical cooperation, however, has a whiff of integration, the kind of cooperative, nonmarket activity firms do on their own, and the proof that it is anticompetitive usually falls to the authorities.

Horizontal cooperation is generally viewed with suspicion because it seems to reduce competition and, hence, block efficiency and other objectives that competition facilitates. In mergers, after all, the total number of rival firms in the market drops, shifting the market structure toward oligopoly. In joint ventures, the effect can be qualitatively the same, though it is limited to only some activities and is always a less rigid arrangement than a full merger. However, empirical research shows that the efficiency losses from horizontal cooperation may be quite small as long as three to five rivals remain in a market.[46] And horizontal cooperation can be defended for the efficiencies it may deliver (e.g., a so-called efficiency defense may be based on cost reduction through information sharing and productivity improvement, avoidance of wasteful duplication of fixed costs of research and development, reduction of coordination problems in industrywide rationalization, and facilitation of exit of inefficient firms).[47]

Vertical cooperation is often considered acceptable if rival firms have equivalent opportunities to cooperate and integrate. In this view, equal opportunity vertical cooperation is just another example of free entry— in this case, entry to an organizational structure that spans several production stages. There are, nevertheless, grounds for concern if completely new firms face higher vertical-integration costs than do established incumbents, because the new firms' entry is then limited. This condition is fairly common, for example, when a new entrant needs to build an integrated distribution network from scratch, or when long-term, almost indefinite contracts and buyer loyalty leave a new entrant with no uncommitted suppliers or distributors. These concerns, of course, have animated Japan-US relations, especially in autos, auto parts, and semi-

---

46. See Bresnahan and Reiss (1991) and the appendix to this book. The question regarding merger approval that occupies governments' procedural guidelines is how to define a market for purposes of counting rival firms and evaluating the competitive intensity of the rivalry. If markets are broadly defined (say, chemical products), there are many rivals. If markets are more narrowly defined (say, pharmaceuticals), there are fewer; if still narrower (say, aspirin), even fewer. The narrower the definition, the more likely that governments will find market power and its various abuses.

47. Sometimes called the failing-firm defense. Dick (1997) finds evidence of efficiency gains even among US export cartels.

conductors. In the anticompetitive extreme, vertical arrangements among firms may completely choke off comparable entry by rivals. This so-called vertical foreclosure is agreed to be anticompetitive and should be subject to intense competition-policy scrutiny. The classic example of such entry foreclosure is an exclusive contract between incumbent firms and suppliers of some vital input for which there is no substitute—for example, a deposit of ore or diamonds of the purest quality. A more recent, yet controversial, example may be the exclusive, 20-year contracts that Boeing negotiated with American Airlines, Continental Airlines, and Delta Air Lines to be their sole supplier. At least the competition-policy authorities of the European Union thought it was an example; Boeing responded that there was nothing that kept Airbus from competing for these or similar contracts (reports were that they did), and, hence, there was no foreclosure. As noted earlier in this chapter, to gain approval for its merger with McDonnell Douglas, Boeing agreed not to enforce the exclusivity of the contracts but at the same time changed none of their other terms.

Still more controversial gray-area practices include vertical arrangements that enhance price-setting and price-discrimination power, such as those of a manufacturer that prevents its distributors from either independently discounting its products (resale price maintenance) or from remarketing them outside the distributor's designated territory.[48] While such restrictions are anticompetitive because they ban entry by distributors into the business of arbitrage, they also procompetitively support a manufacturer's ability to: ensure local maintenance and repair services, charge an appropriate price for services offered to distributors (avoiding free riding by unauthorized distributors), and charge different prices in different regions, at different times, or to different customers. These types of price discrimination can sometimes promote efficiency when they expand markets or open new ones (while admittedly sacrificing some fairness).

Open-Economy Considerations

Horizontal and vertical cooperation both work differently in an open economy than in a closed one. One reason is that governments represent only their domestic constituents, whereas markets pull firms and customers together across national borders. Collusion may actually be attractive to a government if foreign customers or foreign rivals bear most of

---

48. See Scherer (1994, 74-75) for a discussion of the EU competition authorities case against Grundig. The authorities at one time prevented Grundig's distributors in one EU member country from shipping its electronics products into another (shipments called parallel imports). Less extremely, Canadian and US auto dealers face different tariffs than do the resident producers of the cars.

the efficiency and equity burdens. That is why many governments allow export cartels that fix prices, restrain attribute competition, divide up markets, and engage in other activities that are usually prohibited domestically. That is also why governments sensibly restrict the rights of foreign firms to join standard-setting or research consortiums (such as the US joint venture Sematech). And that is why many governments favor mergers of domestic firms that enhance their firms' global market power, even though the governments' constituents bear some of the costs. For example, that is one possible reason why US authorities might look more favorably on the merger of Boeing and McDonnell Douglas than do European authorities (though US authorities deny it). Or, for example, a vertical merger between two home firms that impedes the entry of foreign rivals can enhance not just a firm's market power, but national market power and the national standard of living as well. (Entry to the US market by oligopolistic and integrated European suppliers was an understandable concern of the United States in recent WTO negotiations over basic telecommunications services.) Of course, in all these cases much of what one country gains is lost by others, engendering conflict and the opportunity for international conflict resolution to discipline these beggar-thy-neighbor competition policies. More ambitiously, international cooperation over trade and competition policies could provide the opportunity to come closer to global efficiency.

Avoiding opportunistic policies is not the only reason for government-to-government agreements concerning relational practices in an open economy. Mergers in one country can often cause inefficiencies or inequities in another, even through exports rather than on-site operations. Thus, a given merger must often clear several different competition-policy reviews, as illustrated by the European Union review of the proposed merger between Boeing and McDonnell Douglas. Some governments have negotiated information-sharing agreements in their merger review procedures, yet one of the contentious issues raised by the Boeing-McDonnell Douglas case is whether an offshore review should defer to a primary review (in this case, by the United States) when the assessments differ. In this case the European Union pressed on anyway, even in the face of US approval, and Boeing eventually made concessions. Within the European Union, large mergers, meeting other criteria, are evaluated at the community level, not by national authorities.

Although open economies may lead to some inefficiencies, they may also magnify the size of efficiency gains from interfirm cooperation, when such gains are there and distribute those gains to all countries. Opportunism is then only an issue in the fair division of the gains. Examples are the on-again, off-again consideration of a joint venture by Boeing and Airbus to build a superjumbo aircraft and joint space research between Russian and US firms.

Some features of an open economy stand in the way of efficient and fair cooperation among firms. Antidumping conventions, implemented at the beginning of the twentieth century to discipline price discrimination in international trade, have metastasized into the weapon of choice against foreign rivals. They are as useful for harassment as for protection and are a facilitator of implicit collusion (Lipstein 1997). Successful antidumping cases are resolved either by erecting inefficient antidumping duties or by allowing firms to negotiate—that is, jointly fix—higher prices (this solution is called a price undertaking). Such sanctioned horizontal collusion raises costs to all users, rations some users, and can slow down innovation. Market-opening tools such as voluntary import expansions (VIEs) and US market-access (Section 301) cases are export analogs to antidumping measures. Whatever procompetitive merit these substitute weapons may have in forcing entry is usually more than offset by their implicit facilitation of cartelization in the target country and collusion at home (Greaney 1996).

Anticompetitive corporate and intercorporate behavior are the immediate concerns of competition policy. But both recur in a longer time frame and in a wider context. We describe the longer time frame as lifetime behavior and the broader context as social behavior.

Lifetime Behavior

Competition policy is also concerned with a firm's long-term market behavior, both individually and in relation to rivals. The key lifetime objectives are efficiency and fairness but with a wider scope than described so far. Efficiency must now include ideal rates of investment, innovation, and attribute introduction that reflect the valuations and varied needs of future buyers—some of whom are not yet discernible or even born. Fairness must now outline the circumstances under which an established firm should be allowed to die, either by absorption into another firm or by liquidation. Efficiency may sometimes dictate the extinction of an entire sector (e.g., television sets), raising especially troublesome fairness questions, especially if the same sector survives in other countries.[49]

So in addition to the classic competition-policy issues enumerated above, this lifetime concern involves extinction, succession, innovation, and change of ownership. These are influenced by policies toward exit and downsizing, bankruptcy and public bailout commitments, education and taxation of research and development, industrial secrets and intellectual

---

49. But is it really sensible to limit a sector to only television sets, rather than consumer electronics or electronics in general? The broader the characterization, the less compelling is the allegation of unfairness, especially when firms are diversified. The United States led the recent push for an Information Technology Agreement (ITA) despite near absence of US domestic production of consumer electronics.

property, and takeovers and corporate control. Long-term competition policy involves implicit assessments of questions such as the following:

- What (if any) recourse should shrinking firms in shrinking industries have to temporary relief from global market pressures, from normal competition policy, and from creditors' repayment schedules?

- How easily can the firm abandon weak product lines or sell them to others? How easily can it abandon inefficient production processes or look to outside suppliers for components?

- How actively does a firm work its intellectual property? Can its favorable market position in current technologies or product varieties allow it to slow down its own innovation or that of rivals? What is the optimal amount of protection to be given to intellectual property to encourage the right amount of innovation?

- How easily can outsiders purchase enough equities to gain control of the firm and alter its basic decisions (free entry in the market for corporate control)?

Schumpeterian Competition

Neither research nor competition-policy precedents are well developed with respect to these questions. Nearly all specialists pay lip service to the conviction of the economist Joseph Schumpeter that innovation and corporate displacement and succession cycles (creative destruction) are the keys to dynamic efficiency. But no one has yet worked out the formal properties of Schumpeterian dynamic efficiency as carefully or persuasively as they have been worked out for point-in-time efficiency (but see Dinopoulos 1994). Hence, competition-policy analysts have relatively little in the way of normative guidelines to design regimes for intellectual property, corporate takeovers, overseas investment, and similar issues.

Other important issues in the social ideal for lifetime behavior are still unresolved. One concerns attribute competition. There is no guarantee, even in theory, that the number of varieties generated by free-market entry of firms into attribute competition (say, the number of fast-food restaurants at a busy intersection) is socially ideal. Markets can in some circumstances create too many varieties (inefficient excessive competition [Suzumura 1997]) or, in other circumstances, too few (also inefficient). Thus, highly contestable markets in attribute competition are not necessarily to be pursued as strongly as highly contestable markets in price and quantity competition.[50]

---

50. We are not persuaded of the practical importance of this, however, leaving us still willing to use contestability as a summary guide to our policy recommendations in chapter 3.

Market Structure and Technological Innovation

What is the effect of market structure on the rate of technological innovation? And what is the appropriate mix of competition policy and intellectual property protection to move that rate toward socially optimal values? The issue is of importance because technological advance is, in the long run, the most important determinant of productivity advances—that is, the rate at which society can increase output without necessarily increasing its tangible inputs.

Most research finds innovation lower at the extremes of perfect competition and perfect monopoly. More precisely, those sectors that are neither highly competitive nor monopolies tend to create and utilize new technology at faster rates than do other sectors (see Scherer and Ross 1990).

The usual story is that firms in highly competitive industries are not good at creating new technologies because technology is a public good and, in particular, because of what is called nonrivalry. The basic idea is that technology, at its fundamental level, is human knowledge; and the quantity of one person's knowledge is not depleted if that person passes on the knowledge to someone else. Hence, knowledge is said to be nonrival.

However, the value of specific knowledge to a person might be reduced by passing it on: If only one person knows how to achieve cold fusion, for example, that person might be able to make a fortune from commercializing this knowledge; if everyone else knows what that person knows, any fortune to be made will be spread among millions of people. In the latter case, everyone benefits from this knowledge—we will have a new source of low cost energy—but no one will become richer than anyone else.

The argument goes like this: if there is considerable competition in a market, no one seller is likely to benefit from developing a new product or new process if the knowledge associated with that development will quickly become known to all other sellers. Indeed, because technological innovation typically is the fruit of costly research and development, the innovating firm might actually be punished, because this firm alone bears the costs, whereas everyone shares the rewards.[51] This situation is generally known as the appropriability dilemma: the innovator cannot appropriate the full value of the knowledge he or she develops and,

---

51. This assumes that the knowledge diffuses from the innovator to the other firms without cost, an assumption that will not generally hold. Indeed, some highly innovative firms proceed on the assumption that rivals will not be able to easily replicate knowledge generated within the innovative firm or that the time between innovation and imitation will be sufficiently large that, by the time rivals have mastered the knowledge, the innovator will have moved on to still newer innovations.

indeed, the amount that is appropriated by the innovator might not warrant the irrecoverable (sunk) costs incurred to create the knowledge. The appropriability dilemma has a social dimension: the value of the new knowledge to society (including both sellers and buyers in the relevant market) might be much higher than the costs of developing the knowledge; however, if no one can appropriate enough of this total value to cover research and development costs, the knowledge will never be generated.

The appropriability dilemma is the major economic justification for intellectual property protection; that protection is a deviation from normal competition policy. It gives the innovator a limited monopoly right to work a new technology and, hence, to increase the total appropriable value of this technology.

Advocates of strong intellectual property protection argue that the stronger this protection is, the more that can be appropriated and the stronger the incentive to innovate. This argument cannot be easily dismissed. However, the stronger this protection is, the slower will be the diffusion of new technology from the innovator to other firms (which may then improve upon it). Thus, many economists argue that too much intellectual property protection can be a bad thing by lowering the overall rate of adoption of new technologies, which depends on both innovation and diffusion (and on the improvements that often accompany diffusion). Theory and empirical evidence support this position (Scherer and Ross 1990). Therefore, the socially correct amount of intellectual property protection is, at best, an uncertain matter.

The appropriability dilemma also is invoked to justify cooperation in research and development among sellers who otherwise must compete. If the costs of creating new technology are pooled among sellers, then the disincentive to the innovator from having to bear the full costs while sharing the rewards is reduced. This might result in higher rates of innovation. However, as with intellectual property protection, this conclusion is conditional, as shown below.

Both intellectual property protection and cooperative research and development can be seen as restricting competition. But, as we have stressed, competition policy has, as one of its ultimate objectives, long-term efficiency. Thus, even if competition is reduced if efficiency-enhancing technological innovation is increased, then intellectual property protection and cooperative research and development would be consistent with the objectives of competition policy. However, the "ifs" must be carefully examined: will higher rates of technological advance result? Again, there is no strong, normative guideline to help with this examination.

If the appropriability dilemma explains why highly competitive industries do not innovate as rapidly as less competitive ones do, then why do monopolies also tend to be noninnovative? After all, a monopolist does not have to worry about other sellers capturing the rewards of technological innovation. Rather, the monopolist gets all of the reward (or, to be accurate, gets all of the reward that accrues to sellers, because in the absence of perfect price discrimination, some of the reward will be passed to users in the form of additional consumer surplus).[52] From the perspective of the monopolist, the problem is that sinking costs into research and development is to subject oneself to uncertainty: the expenditures might or might not achieve a satisfactory return. And why should the monopolist do this when it already earns monopoly profits? To be sure, if the research and development is successful, profits will increase. But if shareholders are content with current profits, why take the chance that profits will be reduced by unsuccessful efforts at innovation, when to do nothing would be perfectly satisfactory?

Thus, monopolies tend not to be innovative, because there is some risk to spending on research and development but no apparent risk to not spending. Indeed, this reason applies to intellectual property protection and joint research and development ventures: they reduce the appropriability problem but also can reduce the risk of not innovating. In the case of intellectual property, if the protection granted to existing technology is too great, there will be little or no risk that a rival firm will usurp market share by bringing to the market a still better version of this technology. In the case of joint ventures, the temptation might be for all firms to act more like monopolists than innovative risk takers.

It is often argued that in all of these cases the antidote is to make it risky not to perform research and development. This is best accomplished by introducing competition or, at least, contestability in the market. If there is significant risk that, in the event that an incumbent monopolist does not innovate, an innovative entrant will take away market share, then the incumbent will have to balance the risks of doing research and development against the risks of not doing it. And, if there is potential for product or process improvement (and in what sector is there not?), the likely decision will be to undertake the costs and risks of innovation.

The upshot is that an innovative industry is likely to be quite contestable, but innovative firms can still expect to capture significant rewards. This suggests a market structure that is monopolistically competitive, with only fleeting advantages held by the successful innovator. However, the

---

52. There is a third reward that might be generated by technological innovation, via the creation of so-called positive externalities. Suppose, for example, that the innovation is a better and cheaper device to clean automotive exhaust, which ultimately improves air quality significantly. Then anyone who can stop taking drugs to combat respiratory problems created by the now eliminated smog is a beneficiary of this innovation via this externality: they benefit, but they do not pay.

structural determinants of whether an industry is innovative are not wholly understood.[53]

One result is that competition policy does not deal wholly with issues of innovation nor, indeed, with the panoply of lifetime issues facing a firm. Indeed, competition policy does no more than sanction three rather ad hoc institutions: exceptions (or, at minimum, looser regulation) for joint ventures for research and development; monopolistic intellectual property protection regimes; and forbearance for recession and rationalization cartels. The idea in the first two is to reduce the cost of entry for new products and processes and to improve conditions for appropriability; the idea in the third is to reduce the cost of exit for the old, thus encouraging Schumpeterian dynamic efficiency.

With respect to the third, there are few studies to indicate whether these cartels really do reduce the cost of exit. Nonetheless, we suggest experimentation with these and other competition-policy safeguards, because they are more efficient (and often more equitable) than trade remedies (antidumping and countervailing duties) in downsizing activities in which a country's producers have lost comparative advantage.

With respect to innovation, it is clear that markets alone tend to undersupply new technology, but it is not yet clear how competition policy can help the market overcome its shortcomings. The recent commitment by all WTO members to historically established systems of intellectual-property protection is an intriguing real-life institutional experiment in policies to encourage dynamic efficiency.[54] Whatever its outcome, in 20 or more years many questions will remain about the optimal design of such institutions, such as how long-lived such protection should be and how broad its coverage should be across varieties of similar innovations.

Globalization, Governance, and Cross-Border Investment

Though competition policy is rarely defined so broadly as to include issues of corporate governance, cross-border investment and trade increasingly force the two together in evaluating the lifetime behavior of firms. Thus, for example, cross-border investment can be a vehicle for

---

53. For example, traditional 20-year protection of patentable inventions might seem long rather than fleeting. More generally, the issue of the ideal length of patent protection and of patent scope (does the patent cover major variations of a new technology or only minor ones?) is not well addressed by economic reasoning. One consequence is that patent life and scope has been determined by historic precedent rather than by reason and evidence.

54. This commitment is embodied in the TRIPs agreement. Proponents of this agreement believe that its implementation will encourage the diffusion of technology to nations that, in the past, international investors have been reluctant to transfer technology to because of weak intellectual property protection. Critics, however, worry that full implementation of TRIPs could lead to overzealous protection of intellectual property with the deleterious effects (already noted above).

both new entry of products and for innovation.[55] Japanese investment in North American steel, rubber, and auto assembly facilities, for example, reestablished US compact-car production and revolutionized US factory organization.[56] Thus, policies that encourage cross-border investment may facilitate the goal of contestability (Graham 1996a, chapter 4). Among other such policies are commitments to rights of establishment and national treatment for foreign firms and disciplining of discriminatory performance requirements that were not covered by the Uruguay Round Trade-Related Investment Measures (TRIMs). But brokerage, forecasting, risk assessment, and risk management are among the important supports and complements to these investment policies. All of these support policies are an informational infrastructure to make global investment markets work efficiently and fairly, much as competition policy is a national infrastructure with the same objectives.

Social Behavior

Competition policies are almost always modulated and influenced by broader social objectives.

Sectoral and Corporate Differences

Because it often clashes with other objectives, competition policy varies across sectors. Competition policy is usually tailored to sectoral public-interest regulation—especially in transportation, telecommunications, and utilities—and often tailored to industrial policies that favor agriculture or high-technology sectors over others. Competition policy is almost always made subservient to national-security considerations in defense contracting and defense-sector downsizing.[57] Competition policy has never been applied indiscriminately to financial markets nor to labor markets where labor unions compete with each other and with company representation to represent workers collectively (cooperatively, and collusively). Occasionally, competition policy even differentiates among competing firms, with state-owned or state-chartered firms treated with more leniency (but this differential treatment is not sanctioned in either Europe or North America).

---

55. See Noland (1997) for a negative assessment of the hypothesis that cross-border investment is restrained by anticompetitive entry deterrence practices.

56. Most Japanese investment in steel and rubber involved taking over failing firms; most auto investment involved greenfield investment (building plants from the ground up). Entry was obviously higher than otherwise in the latter case but also higher in the former, because exit of US firms, which would have happened without the investment, was allayed.

57. See, for example, Linking Arms: A Survey of the Global Defense Industry, *The Economist*, 14 June 1997, 7-8.

Functional Differences

Competition policy is also altered to serve social goals without regard to sector. Examples are the promotion of small or minority-owned businesses, maintenance of indigenous culture, assurance of service to peripheral or declining subregions, and buttressing of government revenue. For example, small businesses in some countries (e.g., France and Japan) are protected by distribution laws that allow mom-and-pop retailers to block the arrival of a new (and often larger) entrant (see Jenny 1997; Matsushita 1997). Examples of the policies that maintain indigenous culture are special barriers to ownership of publishing enterprises and mass media by foreigners and, hence, barriers to mergers that involve them (see Goldman, Bodrug, and Warner 1997), and antitrust exemptions for local sports (e.g., North American baseball). Until recently, telecommunications and other utilities illustrated policies that support universal service. Firms in these sectors have been allowed to maintain privileged positions of market power in exchange for their pledge to serve the hinterlands, financing that otherwise unprofitable service with excess profits earned from their entry-protected positions.[58] An example of the policies that buttress government revenue is the willingness of governments to compromise competition-policy objectives when privatizing a state-owned monopolist—government revenues from the sale are kept higher when the government guarantees the same privileged market position to the private buyer.

When competition policy differs for these reasons across sectors, firms, regions, or activities, efficiency and fairness of the normal sort suffer, as described in the next section. That is the tradeoff for or price of meeting other social objectives. However, some commentators argue that this price is rising all too rapidly because of the weakness of existing competition policies (see Rosenthal and Nicolaidis 1997). And when countries differ in the sectors, firms, regions, or activities that they exempt for social reasons, efficiency and fairness suffer at the global level as well. Conflict over the fairness of differing exceptions becomes inevitable.[59]

Economywide and Worldwide Concerns of Competition Policy

The efficiency and fairness concerns of competition policy are different when viewed from a distance rather than from a sector's vantage point.

---

58. The sanctioned financing is called cross-subsidization. But in the United States and elsewhere, deregulation and international market opening are allowing entry to undercut these cross-subsidies and forcing regulators to find less anticompetitive means to subsidize service in remote regions.

59. Suzumura (1997) outlines the types of considerations that might go into deciding permissible exemptions policies.

There are unique insights about the forest that do not characterize the trees.

Economywide and Worldwide Efficiency

Efficiency is achieved by a somewhat different set of guidelines for the economy as a whole than for a single sector or firm. One of the things that matters most for single industries or firms is the relationship of output prices to input costs for given product attributes. But what matters for economywide efficiency are relative prices and costs from sector to sector. At any point, an economy is reasonably efficient if:

- the prices of goods and services from sector to sector have the same relative values as under perfect competition, whether or not this extreme form of competition really exists and whether or not the prices are close to costs, and

- input costs are the same from sector to sector and firm to firm, rather than, for example, being cheaper to incumbents or to favored firms or sectors.[60]

That relative prices and costs are what really matter for economywide efficiency has some surprising implications. The fundamental implication is that, with one important exception, a single economy can still be reasonably efficient when each of its sectors faces comparable competitive imperfections (e.g., if each sector is populated by the same set of rival incumbent firms that block out newcomers and charge prices that are marked up comparably over costs, say, by 30 percent).[61] The economy is still reasonably efficient because excess profits and barriers to entry are roughly the same throughout the economy; there is no economywide incentive to underproduce in one sector relative to another, and the sector-by-sector mix of goods available to buyers is close to that which perfect competition would generate (because the product prices of each sector relative to others are also the same as under perfect competition).[62]

---

60. Favored firms might include those with public ownership or ownership by ethnic minorities or firms with a license to unique resources or with political connections. Favored sectors often include those with prominent places in a development plan, or those meeting social objectives. Price discrimination by input suppliers creates differences across buyer firms, which is presumptively inefficient (Varian 1989, 623-24), unlike price discrimination by final-goods suppliers.

61. This outcome is sometimes described as the "equal degree of monopoly" environment. See Scherer and Ross (1980, appendix to chapter 2).

62. British competition law actually seeks a "balanced distribution of industry" (Hay 1997).

The important exception to this economywide efficiency is that the relative prices of new products, processes, or technologies that would have often been produced by the blocked, nascent newcomers as their ticket to successful entry may be wrong. Product innovation will, as a result, usually be too low, as will the number of product varieties. Process innovation may also be too low, because the costs of new processes are distorted, and entrants with new ideas for how to produce products are also blocked.[63]

This insight on economywide efficiency is less abstract than it may appear. Economies such as South Korea's, in which the same corporate conglomerates (called *chaebol*) compete across virtually all industries, may not have egregious inefficiencies and distortions in any particular sector (except innovation)—as long as South Korea remains reasonably insulated from the world economy. And economies such as Germany's, in which powerful labor unions bargain nationally and represent workers across many sectors, may not have egregious sectoral inefficiencies and distortions—except in innovation and except as the sharp market competition from the rest of the world impinges indirectly on German labor market power.[64] By contrast, economies with sectorally uneven market power (e.g., government-sanctioned monopolies in transport or telecommunications) often have more inefficiency—visibly bad quality, slow service, and high prices—in those sectors (but they are not so inefficient in other sectors).

Even in an economy with sectorally even market power, however, a lack of innovation might cause static inefficiency to grow over time. This is because innovation itself is uneven across sectors and, hence, causes relative prices to change. An economy that is insulated from such changes will become increasingly inefficient even in the static sense. Additionally, because new technologies will be adopted elsewhere and not at home, producers in the insulated economy will become increasingly technologically inefficient. Put in plain English, they will become backward by failing to adopt technological improvements. The economies of Eastern Europe and the Soviet Union during the 1970s and 1980s are examples. Dominance of these economies by state-owned monopolies led both to increasing static (allocational) inefficiency due to relative price distortions as well as to technological backwardness. One consequence

---

63. A less important exception is that the price of leisure may be distorted, because it cannot meaningfully be produced by the same monopolistic mark-up process. See Scherer and Ross (1980, appendix to chapter 2). Leisure may be either underproduced (excessive labor supply) or slightly overproduced (insufficient labor supply), with the latter slightly more likely according to empirical estimates of the wage elasticity of the labor supply.

64. The same might be said to be the result of inefficient distribution systems across all sectors in Japan.

was a high level of so-called x-inefficiency or, in other words, overstaffing (and featherbedding) in the state-owned enterprises.

However, technological backwardness and increasingly inefficient allocation of resources do not necessarily follow if the economy is at least open to imports of technology. South Korea again serves as an example. Although during the 1970s and 1980s it was relatively closed to imports of goods and (nonfactor) services, South Korea was not closed to imports of technology. In fact, Korean firms—including the *chaebol*—paid large fees to gain access to new technologies. One result was that relative prices in South Korea changed in response to technological improvement, and another was that South Korean firms technologically caught up with their rivals in the rest of the world. Also, these firms diversified into new activities, often those where technological advances were occurring most rapidly. Overall, South Korea's economic position in the world (as measured by per capita GDP) rose, at exactly the same time that the position of most of Eastern Europe fell.

For similar reasons, inefficiency is also high in economies in which the cost of the same resource differs dramatically from firm to firm or from sector to sector, say, because of government favoritism or ethnic or family connections. But inefficiency is not necessarily high in insulated economies where everyone faces the same input prices, even if input prices are altered by heavy regulation or taxation (e.g., payroll taxes).

This insight on economywide efficiency is, more precisely, that

- point-in-time (static) efficiency for an economy in isolation does not require perfect competition; it can be approached when there are competitive distortions that are pervasive yet comparable across activities.

Six more insights follow directly:

- The same economy is likely to be dynamically inefficient: it may not grow quickly if its structure discourages product and process innovation by new firms.

- Efficiency may be ensured, but not fairness of opportunity; new entrants are uniformly shut out.

- The economy's apparent efficiency may fade as it opens to world markets; every sector in the economy and every input market will be pressured by global counterparts whose corresponding sectors are organized more competitively.

- The greatest pressure will come in the most dynamic sectors—that is, the sectors or input markets that are most innovation-intensive.

- Pressures from global rivals may appear unfair because their economies do not tolerate any modulation or cushioning of ruthless efficiency-enhancing competitive forces.

- Increasingly integrated global financial markets are catalysts for these competitive pressures, creating both opportunity and risk. Efficient corporate cooperation, labor relations, and regulation (e.g., prudential regulation of the financial markets) will actually be rewarded; it is not inevitable that conglomerates and social market economies are eclipsed.

These insights need further discussion, for example, in the working party of the WTO that is now studying them.

One important implication of these insights is that setting an efficient regulatory baseline is a crucial precondition for defining anticompetitive practices. In the long run, there will be no avoiding the need for governments to sit down to negotiate and then recognize efficient competition-policy rules for permissible interfirm cooperation and even for permissible organization of labor markets.[65] Such internationally recognized rules will define (and deliver) baseline efficiency for all countries that agree to them and for all sectors that are covered. The baseline may look inefficient relative to some other norm or relative to some definition of efficiency that puts more weight on its dynamic character than its static character (efficiency for growth or for current generations), but arguing over such differences and experimenting with and monitoring alternative baselines will be a crucial part of the process.

Economywide and Worldwide Fairness

Fairness, likewise, is also achieved somewhat differently for the economy as a whole than for each sector. One important reason is that many firms, large and small, are diversified across sectors (large firms that produce in many sectors are called conglomerates). Thus, sectoral differences in competition policy may not be unfair to any particular (diversified) firm. For example, a division of a conglomerate such as General Electric may decide to enter a new line of production such as broadcasting (General Electric owns the National Broadcasting Company [NBC]). Thus, General Electric is less vulnerable from an economywide perspective than from the perspective of the electrical-equipment industry alone—

---

65. These will inevitably involve worker rights to cooperate—that is, organize and collectively transact (bargain), which are rights that mirror the rights of firms to do the same. However, efficient foundational rules would almost surely make union representation more contestable than it is in most countries, reducing the market power of incumbent unions and easing the potential of new-entrant unions to displace inefficient incumbents. Cross-border trade in union organization and representation is a still more distant instrument for achieving efficient foundational labor-relations rules, but it has the same economic rationale as all cross-border competition. Free trade in union representation enhances the contestability of labor markets and has rewards in both efficiency and (arguably) fairness!

it is a diversified incumbent. And, correspondingly, if it were forced to leave one of its many lines of business, perhaps even by predation from another diversified conglomerate, the inequity seems less compelling if some of its workers, efforts, and rewards are simply reoriented to its other product lines.

This insight also has valuable implications for international conflict. Fairness-motivated competition-policy conventions may be less needful when the underlying constituents are sectorally diversified multinational companies like Daewoo, Mitsubishi, Philip Morris, and Siemens. Reciprocated entry (cross-penetration) by such firms into each others' diverse domestic markets may make the prototypical global market monopolistically competitive rather than oligopolistic. There would be less need for competition policy of any kind to the extent that market power and its abuse are more tightly constrained by the former market structure than by the latter. Diversified multinational firms can take care of themselves. But market competition among them can take care of disciplining any abuses of market power they may contemplate. The apparent power of each is illusory, undermined by the strong competition of the others.[66]

Smaller firms, however, or those that produce only a single product or handful of products, may be less insulated. So competition policy is more needful with them in mind, especially if small firms can be disproportionately large agents of entry and innovation. However, the large multinationals often relate vertically to hundreds of small, specialized, domestic suppliers whose need for fair and efficient treatment in global markets is taken care of by the implicit representation of their large corporate customers, not by policy. The place for policy, however, may naturally remain, to discipline abuses of market power among large and small firms whatever their nationality.

Finally, fairness can often be achieved among a few large firms by negotiation alone. The transactions costs of negotiating are generally lower the fewer the agents represented. Thus, there is no need for an elaborate fairness policy if firms can work out their perceived inequities (and potential inefficiencies) through legal joint ventures and other cooperation.[67] This simply illustrates the good kind of interfirm relation described above.

---

66. Global cartelization or implicit collusion among these multinationals, such as took place in the 1930s, is clearly to be avoided. This is another natural task of an international competition-policy regime.

67. But there is still a need for competition policy to define the boundaries of cooperation legally and to enforce those boundaries clearly.

3

Implications for Trade and Investment Policy

Cross-national differences in competition policies are likely to pose increasingly significant obstacles to global trade and investment, thus causing growing inefficiencies in global markets, as outlined in chapter 2. Conflict over competition policies is almost always due to differences in perceived fairness; the inefficiencies will grow as investment and services liberalization leaves uncompetitive firms exposed, and as changes in technology and communications make all markets more global.

This chapter traces the policy implications of the economic fundamentals presented in chapter 2, using the twin criteria of desirability and feasibility.

Our conclusion is that there is wisdom and promise in both active cooperative and unilateral efforts to alleviate conflict over competition policies. Specifically, we propose multilateral action on a market-access-oriented subset of Trade-Related Antitrust Measures (TRAMs). We also believe that these efforts, if successful, will establish the networks and trust for a more challenging endeavor—the development of competition-policy safeguards for declining industries, which would be preferable to antidumping mechanisms and subsidies in the eyes of most constituencies. These would allow some existing procedures to be rationalized and others to be phased out.

The Issues: Desirability and Feasibility

Drawing from chapter 2 and the various studies in Graham and Richardson (1997), we have identified the priority trade and investment issues in international competition policies and grouped them in tables 1 and 2.

Table 1 Criteria for a global competition-policy agenda: detail

	Economic clarity	State of convergence		Feasibility of further convergence[b]	Gains from further convergence[b]	
		Toward best practice	Toward each other		Efficiency gains	Conflict reduction
Issues pertaining to market structure						
Cartelization	Clear	Low	High	Moderate	High	Moderate/high
Unwarranted horizontal restraints	Clear	Moderate	Moderate	Moderate	High	Low/moderate
Vertical arrangements						
Resale price arrangements	Murky	Controversial[a]	Low	Moderate	Low	Low
Foreclosure	Murky	Controversial[a]	Low	Low	Moderate	High
Strategic alliances	Murky	Controversial[a]	Low	Indeterminate	Moderate	Indeterminate
Mergers and acquisitions regulation	Clear minus	Moderate	Moderate	Moderate/high	Moderate	Moderate
Issues pertaining to firm conduct						
Predation	Clear minus	Controversial[a]	Moderate	Low	High	High[b]
Price fixing	Clear	High	High	High	High	Low
Price discrimination	Clear minus	Controversial[a]	Moderate	Low/moderate	Low	High
Abuse of market power	Murky	Controversial[a]	Low	Low	Indeterminate	Low
Exemptions						
Functional (e.g., for research and development)	Murky	Controversial[a]	Moderate	Moderate	Low/moderate	High
Sectorial (e.g., telecommunications)	Murky	Controversial[a]	Moderate	Low but improving	Moderate	High
Temporal (e.g., for recession cartels)	Murky	Controversial[a]	Low	Moderate	Moderate	Moderate
Efficiency defense	Murky	Controversial[a]	Low	Low	Indeterminate	Moderate

Trade policy measures raising competition concerns

VERs, OMAs, etc.	Clear	Low	Low	High[b]	High	Moderate
VIEs	Clear minus	Moderate	Low	Indeterminate	High	High
Antidumping	Clear	Low	Low but increasing	Low	High	High
National treatment issues						
For imports	Clear	High	High	In place	Low	Low
For foreign direct investors	Clear	Moderate	Moderate but decreasing	Moderate	Moderate/high	Moderate but increasing
Other related issues						
Intellectual property protection	Murky	Controversial	Moderate but becoming higher	Moderate/high[c]	Moderate	High
State aids to industry/subsidies						
Research and development	Murky	Controversial	Low	Moderate[c]	Moderate	Moderate/high
Production	Clear minus	Moderate	Low	Moderate[c]	Moderate	Moderate/high

a. Best practice is not clearly delineated or is controversial.
b. Toward each other or toward best practice.
c. Based on successes and failures in GATT negotiations during the Uruguay Round.

Table 2 Criteria for a global competition-policy agenda: summary

		State of convergence			Gains from further convergence[b]	
	Economic clarity	Toward best practice	Toward each other	Feasibility of further convergence[b]	Efficiency gains	Conflict reduction
Issues pertaining to market structure	Clear minus	Moderate	Moderate	Moderate	Moderate	Moderate
Issues pertaining to firm conduct	Clear minus	Controversial[a]	Moderate	Low	Moderate	Moderate
Exemptions	Murky	Controversial[a]	Low	Moderate	Moderate	High
Trade policy measures raising competition concerns	Clear	Low	Moderate	Moderate	High	High
Other related issues	Murky	Controversial[a]	Moderate	Moderate	Moderate	High

a. Best practice is not clearly delineated or is controversial.
b. Toward each other or toward best practice.

The first column in each table classifies the issue under market structure, firm conduct, exemptions, trade policy, or other. These issue areas are not always mutually exclusive, just as our four-part breakdown among firm behavior, relational behavior, lifetime behavior, and social behavior was not. Nonetheless, we put substantively similar issues in separate categories if the typical regulatory process treats them separately. Table 1 summarizes our provisional categorization in full detail. Table 2 crudely averages table 1 into five rows for each of the five broad issues.

The second column in each table categorizes these issues by chapter 2's criterion of economic clarity—whether there is strong consensus among economists on what is substantively best practice. If there is such a consensus, we label the issue clear; if there is no such consensus, we label the issue murky. On issues where there is a majority consensus but also a minority of specialists who disagree with the consensus, we place the label clear minus.

If there is to be any sort of international convergence on the issues listed, the best practice with respect to the issue should be clear or, minimally, clear minus.[1] If there is no intellectual consensus on what is

---

1. In what follows, note that convergence pertains both to convergence among the laws and policies of nations (necessary if any sort of international accord is to be reached) and convergence between trade policy and competition policy positions on issues where there

the best practice, international convergence would serve no function or, possibly worse, could be counterproductive (i.e., what is the point of converging on a bad practice?).

The remaining columns describe aspects of convergence with respect to each practice. The columns labeled state of convergence describe the status quo; the columns labeled feasibility of further convergence and gains from further convergence describe the feasibility and desirability of changing the status quo. Desirability is assessed with respect to reducing both inefficiency and international conflict. The second and third columns record our assessment of the state of convergence, first toward best practice (when a consensus exists) and, second, across national practices.

The fourth column indicates the feasibility of further convergence. Feasibility in this context means political feasibility (i.e., is there any consensus among policy officials and legislatures on what would be normatively better practice?) We classify issues as low feasibility if either (1) there are substantial differences among officials of different nations on desirable practice, or (2) there is a substantial difference between branches of a single government as to desirable practice.[2] If an issue is not characterized by a high or at least moderate level of feasibility in this sense, there is probably little hope at this time for any sort of reasonable convergence.

The fifth column represents an effort to judge what might be gained, in terms of economic efficiency, from moving from the present policy regime to a convergence on best practices. In areas where we judged the substantively best practice to be murky, we attempted to judge the efficiency implications of continuing practices that economists agree lead to inefficiencies. One way of looking at this judgment is to ask: If we could agree on a substantive best practice, and this agreement had economic merit, what would we gain? The final column indicates for which issues we judge that success in reaching any sort of convergence will lead to conflict resolution. Several issues are labeled at least moderate for three of the following: clarity, feasibility, efficiency, and conflict reduction. The common thread through most of them is market access, and virtually all involve barriers to the contestability of markets. Those issues are

■ cartelization;

■ other horizontal restraints;

---

is substantial overlap (e.g., predation and antidumping). Presumably, what is desired is convergence (in both contexts) toward best practice rather than convergence for its own sake!

2. For example, trade policy officials may defend existing antidumping statutes, but competition policy officials may see these as irrational when evaluated by standards for predation or price discrimination.

- mergers and acquisitions;

- price fixing;

- voluntary export restraints (VERs), orderly marketing arrangements (OMAs), and other similar practice; and

- national treatment for foreign direct investors and services.

Many issues do not make this list but have high efficiency and conflict-reduction implications. These include predation or antidumping and VIEs (for which likely efficiency gains would be substantial if there were political will to implement significant reform of the existing system) (see Itoh and Nagaoka 1997; Lipstein 1997); vertical practices (for which the underlying economics remains murky);[3] intellectual property and related issues (for which the debate over the welfare tradeoff between strong intellectual property protection, and greater rivalry among innovators will likely never be fully resolved); and state aids to industry (Is there such a thing as a good subsidy?). Of these issues, the last three do not make the list because the underlying economics of the issue remains murky and, hence, what is normatively best practice is difficult to determine.

This distillation provides a useful means for categorizing alternative policy recommendations. It provides the substance of a desirable agreement on TRAMs, akin to the current TRIPs and TRIMs measures, and an agenda for reform of some of the least efficient and least equitable aspects of current trade and investment rules.

Alternatives for an International Competition-Policy Process

Our policy recommendations, which focus on contestability and rationalization, are shaped and constrained by desirability and feasibility, as summarized in tables 1 and 2. First, we examine the competition policy issues within the WTO, and conclude that the WTO is at present unable to deal effectively with many of these issues (albeit there are some issues that the WTO can in fact address). Then, we look at alternative ways to fill the gaps, some of which involve the WTO.

Competition Issues within the WTO

The WTO is well equipped to handle certain issues that fall within our definition of competition policy, but it is poorly equipped to handle

---

3. For example, there is room for reasoned debate as to whether vertical *keiretsu* in Japan are efficiency enhancing or otherwise. Sheard (1997) argues, after considering pros and cons, that efficiency-enhancing effects dominate on balance.

others. For example, national obligations under the WTO, combined with WTO dispute settlement mechanisms, proscribe certain government measures that might be deemed anticompetitive. These include, VERs, OMAs, VIEs, and similar measures banned under the Uruguay Round agreements. Likewise, under the General Agreement on Tariffs and Trade (GATT) Article III (national treatment), governments are prohibited from placing discriminatory legal or regulatory burdens on exports if those burdens would not be borne by similar domestically produced products.

Indeed, some basis for attacking any government measure that might have the effect of denying market access to nonincumbent exporters is to be found in GATT Article XXIII. The first paragraph of this article reads as follows:

> If any (member nation) should consider that any benefit accruing to it directly or indirectly under this Agreement is being nullified or impaired or that the attainment of any objective of the Agreement is being impeded as the result of (a) the failure of another (member nation) to carry out its obligations under this Agreement, or (b) the application by another (member nation) of any measure, whether or not it conflicts with the provisions of this Agreement, or (c) the existence of any other situation, the (aggrieved member nation) may, with a view to the satisfactory adjustment of the matter, make written representations or proposals to the other (member nation or nations) which it considers to be concerned. Any (member nation) thus approached shall give sympathetic consideration to the representations or proposals made to it.

The second paragraph of the article allows a member nation that believes that any benefit has indeed been "nullified or impaired" and that the grievance has not been worked out via consultation to invoke the WTO dispute settlement procedures. Given that export foreclosure can in most instances be couched as nullification or impairment of a "benefit accruing . . . directly or indirectly under this Agreement," any government measure that has the effect of closing markets to exports would seem to be covered by this provision. This is because item (b) in the text above seems to imply that any government measure, whether explicitly a trade policy measure or not, is covered by the article. Indeed, the US complaint against Japan currently before the WTO pertaining to access to the Japanese photographic film and paper markets is based, inter alia, on GATT Article XXIII.1.b.[4]

Although the rules of the WTO can cover government measures that impede market access, the same cannot be said of the WTO's ability to cover private measures that have the same effect. The same GATT article (Article XXIII) contains item (c), which, on a casual reading, might seem general enough to be applicable to private measures. However, in 1960, the WTO member nations (or, as they were termed then, the GATT

---

4. Also cited in the US complaint are alleged violations of GATT Articles III (national treatment) and X (transparency).

contracting parties) adopted a recommendation by a working group that Article XXIII.1.c should not be the basis for complaints over alleged export foreclosure brought about by private business practices. This recommendation was rooted in the history of the GATT and, in particular, in the failure to ratify the 1947 Treaty of Havana to create an International Trade Organization. This treaty, if it had been ratified, would have supplanted the GATT agreement and created a new international organization to administer trade rules and, thus, cover private restrictive business practices. The 1960 recommendation was that GATT Article XXIII should not be used to reintroduce into world trade law provisions that earlier had been explicitly rejected. The adoption of this recommendation by the GATT contracting parties made it a part of world trade law that still stands.

It was further recommended that the disputing parties use the GATT consultation procedures to settle disputes over market access problems resulting from private business practices. These procedures are being used in the photographic film dispute mentioned above.

In our view, the 1960 recommendation was wise. The language of Article XXIII.1.c is unspecific and the article provides no guidance whatsoever on difficult issues such as the tradeoff between reduced market access as occasioned by a vertical arrangement and the efficiency-enhancing possibilities created by the practice. Nor, indeed, does it deal with any of the difficult issues of competition policy. Thus, if WTO dispute settlement panels were to decide on cases involving private practices that allegedly impede market access, the decisions would de facto create new rules by precedence on an ad hoc basis. We are not confident that such a process would result in a rational set of rules, and we would seek a better alternative.

The next section examines a number of ways to bring competition policy into the world trading system, including alternatives that do not necessarily involve the WTO.

Three Alternatives

There are three generic means by which competition policy can be carried into international markets to reach situations that fall outside or spill over any particular nation's borders: (1) noncooperative unilateral actions; (2) cooperative unilateral actions (sometimes bilateral, sometimes regional, and sometimes multilateral actions); or (3) variants of supranational mechanisms.

The first alternative is the status quo option. It includes all unilateral actions or efforts undertaken by one nation to redress objectionable practices in some other nation.[5] The shortcomings of noncooperative unilateralism

---

5. For example, efforts to enforce domestic law or policy on the nondomestic activities of firms via some concept of effects doctrine, without working with or through the relevant

are immediately apparent. There is no consensus among national authorities as to what action, if any, is warranted, and if the differences in the objectives of nations are substantial, the actions of one could generate severe frictions. The target might respond with blocking statutes or other measures designed to frustrate the nation initially taking action. Indeed, the final columns of tables 1 and 2 could be seen as a judgment as to how much friction is, or could be, generated by unilateral actions on issues of competition policy.

The third alternative has been implemented within the European Union. Nicolaïdis and Vernon's (1997) conclude that European supranational authority has worked quite well overall. Only a few cases decided by the EU Competition Directorate (DGIV) have led to significant friction within the European Union (e.g., the de Haviland case). However, the European experience is almost surely not repeatable at the international level. The major reason is that early on, the member states of what is now the European Union were willing to allow the European Court of Justice to act as final arbiter of competition policy cases; this court generally has sided with DGIV and, hence, enhanced the powers of this agency. This willingness has allowed competition issues within Europe, to a considerable extent, to transcend national sovereignty. It is unlikely that sovereign states not presently members of the European Union or seeking to become members would be willing at any time soon to cede sovereignty to a supranational agency to a similar extent.

By contrast, the experience of Australia and New Zealand, described by Thomson (1997), suggests some substitutes for supranationality that could be more generally adopted.

This leaves the second alternative, cooperative unilateralism. We believe that this alternative holds much promise.

Cooperative Unilateralism and a Multilateral TRAMs Agreement

Cooperative unilateralism implies that, with cooperative input from other interested authorities, the competition authorities in a nation or region review and, where appropriate, remedy situations within their jurisdictions that might have international ramifications. Such situations include alleged anticompetitive behavior by incumbent firms that impede market access by nonincumbent firms, and mergers whose effects might spill across borders. Two ways that the cooperation might be realized, positive comity and extension of WTO consultations and dispute settlement procedures under a multilateral TRAMs agreement, are considered here.

---

authorities in the nation where the practices actually take place. Both the United States and the European Union (but especially the former) have periodically attempted such an approach.

Positive Comity

Under positive comity, a national government that held a grievance pertaining to another nation's competition policy (e.g., private practices that created barriers to imports or direct investments) would appeal to the authorities of that nation to investigate and, if appropriate, to take action under its own competition laws to address the grievance. In responding to the complaint, these authorities would take into account the interests of the complaining nation. Both NAFTA and the September 1991 Agreement Regarding Application of Their Competition Laws between the United States and the Commission of the European Communities provide guidelines for positive comity.[6]

Positive comity might increase the scope for cooperative investigation and regulation of conduct that crosses national boundaries (e.g., where mergers or alliances were transborder in nature).[7] Thus, for example, the EU's concerns over the Boeing-McDonnell Douglas merger might have led to a joint US-EU review. The same approach might have been used in the auto parts dispute between the United States and Japan (see box 2): the case might have been remanded by trade policy officials to a joint effort between the US authorities and the Japanese Fair Trade Commission.

Extension of WTO (or Other International) Consultation and Dispute Settlement Procedures

Consultation provisions are a natural and necessary companion of positive comity. We believe that there is promising scope for using WTO consultation mechanisms to review implementation of law and policy at the national level. Only a slight broadening of the interpretation of the WTO's existing articles would allow such competition-policy cases to be brought as a type of nullification-and-impairment case that deprives plaintiffs of expected market access.

---

6. See Joelson (1993) in the NAFTA context and Vernon and Nicolaïdis (1997) in the EU-US context. In 1994 the United States adopted a law that would allow the US Department of Justice and the Federal Trade Commission to negotiate mutual legal assistance agreements with foreign antitrust authorities. So far, only Australia has signed such an agreement. Other nations are wary about what they see as excessively aggressive US penal antitrust remedies.

7. More controversially, the rights of firms (including foreign firms) to bring private cases before competition-policy authorities (or the courts) of the relevant country in the case of an alleged violation of its competition laws might be limited. These rights might be made contingent on a demonstration of material injury (even if this injury was of the nature of lost opportunity) to the firm. See, for example, Jackson's similar recommendation (1990, 76-77). Jackson also recommends a filter in the process to reduce spurious complaints. For example, the plaintiff firm's own competition-policy authorities might review the documentation of injury.

However, extending WTO consultation and dispute settlement procedures to competition issues would require minimal rules on what these procedures would cover. This is because the typical complaint brought to the WTO might be that a country allowed a certain practice to persist within its borders and that this practice had trade-related effects (e.g., it foreclosed entry by a firm from some other country). But this would be tantamount to complaining that the country did not enforce its own competition laws—assuming, of course, that such laws exist. WTO panels do not pass judgment on member governments' failure to enforce their national laws and policies where these laws and policies are not germane to specific WTO obligations.[8]

For a panel to do so in the case of competition policy would set a new precedent that member governments would almost surely not be willing to accept. The problem would be greatest in those nations where competition law is largely enforced through judicial proceedings (e.g., the United States), where WTO review of how national law is enforced would be seen as an unacceptable impingement upon national sovereignty and, in particular, upon the powers of the judiciary within a sovereign state.

Therefore, the WTO is much more comfortable with disputes involving putative violation (i.e., failure of a member nation to adhere to an obligation under a WTO agreement) than those involving nonviolation (i.e., nullification and impairment under article XXIII, paragraphs 1[b] or 1[c]). Cognizant of this and the 1960 working group recommendation and following the lead of Fox (1997b), we suggest that a new agreement be negotiated within the WTO.

Fox would label this an agreement on trade-related antitrust measures or TRAMs, in the spirit of the existing agreement on Trade-Related Investment Measures (TRIMs) and (especially) the existing agreement on Trade-Related Intellectual Property (TRIPs). But rather than negotiate a comprehensive agreement pertaining to all aspects of competition policy, Fox proposes that this new agreement focus only on those subdomains that are most relevant to issues of market access. In her judgment, these include

■ cartels with boycotts;

■ vertical arrangements that tend to foreclose outside vendors or block established channels of distribution to new entrants; and

■ monopolistic discriminations and exclusions.

We agree with the approach in principle but disagree with the specifics. Indeed, Fox acknowledges that, while agreement on the first of these

---

8. A government's failure to enforce its own law, where this law reflected a WTO obligation, would, of course, be considered by a WTO panel.

could be relatively straightforward, the second and third are problematic. Vertical arrangements have been ubiquitous to many recent trade disputes. But, as we have noted, these arrangements can also be efficiency enhancing and, indeed, "efficiency defenses" have shielded the so-called production *keiretsu* in Japan, which have been at the heart of many of these disputes (see Sheard 1997). It is largely for this reason that vertical arrangements are, according to our taxonomy of competition issues, murky. Japan, with relaxed policies on vertical arrangements, is at one end of the spectrum, but substantial differences also exist between US and EU doctrine; the United States often accepts efficiency defenses for arrangements prohibited in Europe. Similar differences between the United States and European Union exist in policy toward horizontal market power and resultant monopolistic discriminations and exclusions. For example, with respect to a firm's rights to refuse to deal, US policy allows such refusal by monopolistic firms except under specific circumstances, whereas European policy holds that dominant firms have a duty not to discriminate among customers or refuse to deal.

The point here is that these differences among the three biggest WTO members are sufficiently great as to virtually preclude them from being able to agree on a common set of standards. Also, none of these members have indicated a willingness to relinquish sovereign powers to rule on competition issues to an international body (this is true even of the European Union, even though individual member nations of the European Union do relinquish such powers to the European Commission, an international body).

Thus, we suggest a different specific content to Fox's general TRAMs agreement, focusing on contestability. We would focus on five areas:

- national treatment for local affiliates of foreign firms,
- international control of cartels and cartel-like behavior,
- enlargement of WTO consultative procedures,
- mergers and acquisitions notification, and,
- more speculatively, what we call TRAMs plus.

TRAMS plus is an approach to dealing with declining industries that demand trade protection and might qualify for escape-clause (GATT article XIX) relief. Our proposals in each of these areas provide a positive role for the WTO but do not entail any obligation of WTO members to relinquish sovereign powers to the WTO. Each of these issues is examined in turn.

National Treatment for Local Affiliates of Foreign Firms Much of firms' concern with market access has to do with the right to establish a local presence in a market, and this is typically accomplished by creating (or acquiring) a local subsidiary. In the fast-growing services sectors, such market presence is virtually a prerequisite to international trade in services, a point that has been well recognized in the still unfinished General Agreement on Trade in Services (GATS) of the Uruguay Round. Although not an absolute prerequisite in most manufacturing activities, local market presence is nonetheless highly desirable. These considerations suggest that a vital component of market access is that governments not discriminate against the establishment or operation of a local affiliate of a foreign firm or, in other words, that these affiliates be granted full national treatment.[9]

National treatment for foreign-controlled enterprises is most often thought of as an international investment issue, because lack of national treatment is a major impediment to foreign direct investment. However, any impediment to foreign direct investment is also an impediment to market entry and, hence, to increased market contestability. And, given that increased market contestability is one of the major goals of competition policy, national treatment is also a competition policy issue. Indeed, it might be the competition-policy issue accorded highest priority; many trade-policy issues of market access would simply fade away if governments were to honor an obligation to grant national treatment to foreign controlled firms.

Our own views on how national treatment for foreign controlled enterprises should be implemented have been published in detail elsewhere (see Graham 1996a). Here, we summarize a few points. First, no government is ever likely to endorse full, unqualified national treatment for foreign controlled enterprises, and, hence, there is a practical requirement for a list of exceptions. We believe that, for reasons of transparency, a list of exceptions is preferable to the so-called positive list approach of the GATS, whereby governments commit themselves to granting national treatment of foreign-controlled enterprises for only those sectors that are explicitly listed. We believe that national treatment is not an isolated investment issue that can be dealt with successfully in an agreement that is independent of the WTO agreements. Rather, this is an issue that cuts across trade and investment policy (and is also highly relevant to competition policy). Hence, we do not think that the Multilateral Agreement on Investment (MAI) currently negotiated within the OECD is the correct approach to placing this concept into multilateral trade law, although the OECD work might yield a constructive precursor to a future WTO agreement. Implementation of a WTO agreement on national treatment for foreign-controlled enterprises will likely require some modification of WTO dispute settlement procedures, in particular, some provision for "enterprise to state" dispute settlement.

---

9. This point is developed in Graham (1996a).

On this, the agreement to establish a North American Free Trade Area might provide a useful model (see Graham and Wilkie 1994).

International Control of Cartels and Cartel-like Behavior Virtually all competition policy specialists agree that under most circumstances, cartels are bad. Thus, for almost all nations that have competition laws in place, there are anticartel provisions in those laws. Furthermore, these provisions already largely conform with one another, or, in other words, convergence already exists. It would be relatively easy to achieve international consensus on what we believe to be a priority: a worldwide agreement to ban most cartels.

If many nations already have such a ban in place, why strike an international agreement? There are three reasons. First, not all WTO member nations have competition policies, and, hence, in many nations there are no prohibitions on cartels. Under a WTO agreement, all nations would be required to bring national law into conformity with the agreement. Therefore, the agreement would serve to extend the reach of the ban. Second, enforcement of anticartel provisions has often been lax even in nations with competition laws. A WTO agreement would serve to step up enforcement of these laws, especially where the existence of cartels in one nation create tensions in another nation. Third, some cartels exist purely in international markets, and, indeed, many of these are legal because of various exemptions or loopholes in national laws.

In particular, many nations permit export cartels on the theory that exporters need to have some sort of countervailing power to compete effectively with foreign rivals.[10] However, if every nation allows cartelization of exporters, any national benefit that might accrue is offset by the actions of the cartelized exporters of other nations. All that is left is to share the standard cost of cartels: limits on output and increases in price, to the detriment of buyers of the cartelized product or service. Therefore, we believe that a WTO agreement on cartels should include a ban on most export cartels. There are some exceptions, to be discussed shortly.

As with an agreement on national treatment for foreign controlled enterprises, a WTO agreement on cartels would require some changes in existing dispute settlement procedures. The changes would, fortunately, be rather minor. If a panel, responding to a complaint by a member country, believed that a cartel existed in violation of the agreement, it would recommend that competition authorities in the nation where the alleged violation took place investigate the situation and, where

---

10. The sophisticated version of this is that, if national exporters collectively can exercise market power in foreign markets, they can appropriate rents from foreigners to the benefit of domestic residents.

appropriate, take remedial action. If the authorities failed to do so, the aggrieved nation (or nations) could apply sanctions by following standard WTO procedures.

A thorny issue would occur, however, if the relevant authorities in the violating nation agreed to pursue the case but found in favor of the defendant firm or firms. For example, if the problem were the putative existence of a producers' cartel that boycotted any distributor that handled imported products,[11] the relevant authorities might conclude that no such cartel existed, or that, if it did, its existence did not constitute a violation of national law (in principle, national law would be in conformity with the agreement). In this case, a detailed report would be transmitted to the panel indicating why the authorities reached their conclusion. The panel could be empowered to review the report and determine whether it should be accepted. If it were accepted, the case would be terminated.

But if it were not accepted, withdrawal of WTO concessions (sanctions in the sense used by WTO) might be authorized.[12] Grounds for nonacceptance could be procedural (e.g., the factual investigation had been impaired somehow, or due process was not followed) or substantive (the panel might determine that the relevant national standards were not in conformity with the WTO agreement).

If the report of the authorities was not accepted, however, bolder alternatives than sanctions might be envisaged. One possibility, for example, might be that the panel (or perhaps some other agent) have status to pursue the case in the national courts (or, in the case of the European Union, the supranational courts) of the violating WTO member.

Enlargement of WTO Consultative Procedures   On trade-related issues other than cartels, as we have suggested, there is little likelihood of international agreement on substantive rules to which the above procedures could be applied. There is, however, room for new procedural rules, which could be developed by enlarging existing WTO consultation procedures. As we have already seen, the 1960 GATT decision called for consultation between or among nations if private business practices had alleged effects of foreclosing exports. A simple extension of this would be that WTO member nations be required to enter into consultations over export or investment foreclosure. For purposes of precision, a comprehensive list of private practices, which could be the basis for member countries to request consultations, could be compiled. Inclusion of a private practice on this list would not constitute a prescription against the practice

---

11. As has been alleged, for example, in the case of the flat glass industry in Japan.

12. Fox (1997b) argues for fines rather than sanctions. The WTO presently cannot impose fines, so for Fox's proposal to be implemented, the WTO would have to be given the power to fine members for nonimplementation of panel recommendations.

but only an indication that consultations could be initiated. We believe that such a list should include vertical restraints that might have the effect of foreclosing exports (e.g., exclusive dealing contracts) and monopolistic discriminations as identified by Fox (1997b). But we would enlarge this list and, at the same time, make it more detailed and specific.

Consultations could be bilateral or multilateral, as circumstances dictate. There would be no requirement that the problem be resolved via the consultations. And the consultations would not preclude the use of formal dispute settlement procedures, were these to be applicable to a particular case (indeed, one requirement under these procedures is that the relevant parties attempt to solve a dispute via consultation and negotiation before a panel hears the dispute). Nonetheless, we believe that a considerable number of disputes involving private practices could be resolved via consultation, especially if nations were to proceed in good faith and in the spirit of positive comity.

Mergers and Acquisitions Notification   We advocate mandatory notification for certain mergers and acquisitions likely to have international effects (e.g., mergers between firms having sales outside the home country or countries exceeding certain threshold levels). We envisage that most cross-border mergers or acquisitions would be subject to this requirement. The notification might consist of an announcement that a certain merger or acquisition were pending, publication of basic information regarding the parties to the transaction (e.g., basic income statement and balance sheet information), and indication of whether national authorities of the home country or countries of the parties to the transaction intend to review the merger.

Other countries having a substantial interest in the transaction then could request consultation with those national authorities, as per the mandatory consultation provision outlined above. Substantial interest means that the transaction, if completed, would have material effects in the domestic market of the relevant country. That country's competition officials would determine whether such effects were present. Such a determination would be considered sufficient to show that material effects were present.

Are such procedures for mandatory consultations really necessary? After all, it might be argued, many cases that might have been covered by this procedure (including the Boeing-McDonnell Douglas merger, the US-Japan dispute over auto parts, but not, to date, the US-Japan dispute over photographic film and paper) have in practice been resolved, apparently to everyone's satisfaction, via bilateral procedures. Our response to this argument is that if bilateral or multiparty negotiations can resolve an issue to the satisfaction of all concerned parties, that is fine—but the WTO procedures would be there when and if nations sought to use them. WTO procedures might be utilized more by smaller nations than larger ones, especially if a bilateral resolution were to come at the expense of smaller nations. But WTO procedures might also be used if disputes over merger approval existed among larger nations, especially if more than two nations were to be party to the dispute.

TRAMs Plus: A Competition-Policy Safeguard Mechanism We believe that one more change is possible in the near future, though it is less feasible at the moment than a market-access-oriented TRAMs agreement. As globalization widens and deepens to encompass more regions and more issues (e.g., services), downsizing and rationalization pressures in some sectors will increase as quickly as do opportunities for firms to expand and prosper in other sectors. Ad hoc safeguards such as enhanced antidumping mechanisms (new for many smaller WTO members) and creative subsidization are already burgeoning to cope with the downsizing and rationalization. But these often have high efficiency costs, as shown in chapter 2, and are administered in ways that are at best cumbersome and at worst capricious, creating rancor and inequity.

Competition policies in Japan and parts of Europe have historically handled rationalization and downsizing better (though hardly perfectly), sometimes through functional exceptions such as rationalization cartels and sometimes through sectoral exceptions (e.g., European basic metals). Mergers in which strong firms save weak ones are both efficient and fair if the only other alternative is the extinction of the weak. The most important key to free entry is often rational exit, as described in chapter 2. In that spirit of contestability and market access, we see great potential in a competition-policy-oriented safeguard agreement that could eventually become part of the TRAMs and that would presumably use the same dispute settlement procedures.[13]

For at least two reasons, we think a TRAMs agreement is more feasible than it might appear even from tables 1 and 2. First, cooperative unilateralism and multilateralism along the lines sketched above, will, if successful, build the networks, trust, and precedents for a more ambitious TRAMs agenda. Second, the inefficiencies and inequities of current ad hoc safeguard mechanisms will soon become untenable, as firms and countries that have historically gained from them instead become victims of them at the hands of larger emerging markets and rivals.

A Modest Step Forward, but Not the End of the Road

Our version of the TRAMs proposal is not necessarily the ultimate framework for how competition policy might be implemented at the interna-

---

13. Messerlin (1996), unlike us, sees little merit in a TRAMs agreement except to discipline ad hoc safeguards mechanisms.

tional level, but rather an agenda for a first step in the right direction. As national economies become more and more integrated with one another and business organizations become increasingly global (if, indeed, these trends continue, as we think they will), national governments will likely rethink whether it is in their best interest to retain full sovereignty over competition policy. Quite possibly, governments will continue to be reluctant to cede any authority in this area. However, the world economy could become so integrated that governments begin to see a full-bodied international competition law with a supranational enforcement agency as something that would be in their interest.

However, that time is not now. At present, many policymakers realize that increasing world economic integration poses new challenges for competition policy, but nonetheless are unwilling to cede any national sovereignty. Thus, our TRAMs proposal is meant to be a first, and rather modest step, toward a more international approach to competition policy. The proposal makes maximum use of the existing WTO rules and procedures. Only in two areas would there be substantive new rules, but these are high priority areas where there is already some consensus of views: national treatment for foreign-owned firms and regulation of cartels. Otherwise, what we propose is that national authorities extend a practice they are already engaged in, notably, consultation with one another over specific cases where the interests of more than one national authority are at stake. Additionally, the WTO would be formally notified of certain mergers and acquisitions (so that basic information pertaining to these cases is available to all national authorities), and consultation among national authorities would be mandatory if requested by at least one national authority in a specific case. We believe that implementation of these proposals entails no diminution of sovereign rights of nations nor transfer of national sovereignty to the WTO.

In short, our proposals are meant as a modest first step. Once this step is taken and after enough time passes to allow for some experience with the new procedures, nations can decide on the next step, if there is one. Meanwhile, the first step proposed here is a substantial move in the right direction.

Appendix: Inefficiency, Innovation, Distribution, and Fairness for Suppliers and Demanders in a Globalizing Economy

Figure 1 is a highly simplified, stylized way of illustrating a number of insights from the text of this chapter. The insights are robust in that they remain when the assumptions underlying the figure become more complex, and, hence, the figure becomes less tractable.

Figure 1 shows the efficiency gains that competition policies try to protect and how they are altered by innovation and openness to trade. It shows one type of fairness, fairness over the distribution between sellers and buyers of the economic surplus that market reliance generates (price discrimination especially affects this distribution). It shows the effects of reduced barriers to entry, whether of new firms or new product variants and whether there is domestic entry or entry from abroad.

The curve D represents a nation's overall demand for a standardized product (or a single standardized variant of a differentiated product); the curve MR is the corresponding marginal-revenue curve. These two curves would be the ones used by a nation's firm if it were the only firm serving the national market (that is, if it were a monopolist) and if that market were also closed to trade. When there is more than one supplier firm, whether domestic or foreign, each firm faces (and manipulates and operates on) a firm-specific demand curve and marginal revenue curve that lie inside of and look different than D and MR. When the nation's firms sell abroad, there are a series of other curves like D and MR that represent nation-by-nation demand for the product (variety), all of which need to be added horizontally to D and MR to depict the world demand facing the producers. The elasticity of that worldwide demand curve will be greater than D if, on average, the firms face

Figure 1 Competition policy issues in a stylized global economy

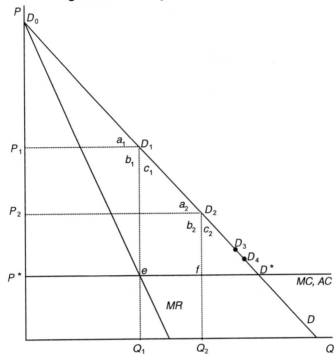

stiffer competition and more elastic demand in export markets than at home.[1] This seems often to be the case (see below). Curve D is drawn straight for convenience, but some conclusions below are altered if that is not so.

For convenience, the curve MC, AC simultaneously represents marginal costs and average costs (total and variable)[2] of the typical firm, domestic or foreign; some conclusions below are altered if that is not so. Furthermore, firms are assumed to be symmetric in their cost curves—that is, identical.

But even with all these restrictive assumptions, figure 1 conveys the flavor of competition policies in the open economy and illustrates many robust conclusions even when the convenient assumptions discussed above are eliminated.

---

1. To be precise, there would be more elastic at every price. The condition is that the sales-share-weighted-average elasticity of export demand be greater than the elasticity of D.

2. Thus, fixed costs are assumed to be zero, and the total cost curve itself is assumed to be linear in the relevant range of Q depicted in figure 1.

For example, one robust conclusion is that "naked" monopoly is far more costly than mere oligopoly (a conclusion that has special application to national champion firms and to the structure of national transportation, telecommunications, utilities, and other regulated industries). Two equilibriums are depicted in detail, D_1 and D_2, corresponding to monopolistic and duopolistic supply (respectively, one supplier and two suppliers) under one of the most common "intermediate" degrees of market imperfection.[3] Equilibriums corresponding to three, four, and a large number of suppliers are indicated in less detail by the points D_3, D_4, and D^*. Most economists agree that the efficiency gains from outlawing naked monopoly are considerably larger than from reducing entry barriers to a third, fourth, or fifth rival. In fact, some evidence (Bresnahan and Reiss 1991) suggests there is little further efficiency gain to be realized once three to five competitors are in place. The robust conclusion that monopoly, not oligopoly, is the real enemy of efficiency can be seen by observing how much smaller triangle c_2 (D_2fD^*) is than triangle c_1 (D_1eD^*).

But what do these areas represent? For many markets, the area of the triangles a_1 $(D_0P_1D_1)$ and a_2 $(D_0P_2D_2)$ measures buyer (or consumer) surplus, the free reward to buyers from the market system—their share of the overall efficiency gains that it generates. The area of the triangles c_1 and c_2 represents inefficiency (deadweight loss), a foregone surplus that could have been captured by buyers or sellers, but is instead sacrificed (wasted) by imperfectly competitive practices. The area of the boxes b_1 $(P_1P^*eD_1)$ and b_2 $(P_2P^*fD_2)$ represents surplus captured by the imperfectly competitive seller that could have been available to the buyer under a more competitive market structure. It is a distributional transfer from buyer to seller and one measure of fairness in a market. It is also a measure of excess (supernormal or economic) profits.

With these interpretations, entry by a new firm not only reduces inefficiency, but also reduces transfers of excess profit from buyers to sellers (b_2 is necessarily smaller than b_1). However, if the new entrant is a foreign firm, then some of box b that used to be transferred to domestic sellers may now go to foreign sellers; that rent shifting (or profit shifting) actually represents a decline in our nation's economic welfare and illustrates one reason why competition policies to reduce entry barriers may be implemented in a discriminatory way: domestic entrants are more welcome on welfare grounds than are foreign entrants.

However, this example also illustrates a central gain from intergovernment cooperation in entry-promoting antitrust initiatives: if two or more competition authorities agree to beat down entry barriers in a nondiscriminatory way, then competitive cross-penetration of the two markets

---

3. Specifically, Cournot competition is being described. See Bresnahan (1989) for an account of its frequently encountered "intermediateness" in empirical practice.

by foreign entrants creates large efficiency gains and transfers to buyers without creating any significant net shifting of rents or profits from one country to the other. Without cooperation, an entry-promoting competition-policy initiative creates both efficiency gains and loss of rents in the zero-sum game between countries. With cooperation, the efficiency gains are enhanced and made mutual, and the win-or-lose, zero-sum aspects of the entry-promoting policy become minimal.[4]

With these interpretations, openness to trade becomes a weapon of competition policy, and the gains from trade grow to include a piece that is attributable to the greater efficiency of market structure. Greater imports often involve new foreign entrants and shift the equilibrium toward the perfectly competitive point, D^*. Greater exports by our firms can also shift the equilibrium toward D^* if they encounter new rivals and stiffer competition in foreign markets, as outlined above.[5]

Furthermore, if either imports or exports expose our firms for the first time to a new range of close substitutes for the product (variant) that we produce, then the whole demand curve D likely becomes more elastic (i.e., flatter, more responsive to price) and this in turn reduces both deadweight loss and arbitrary transfers of surplus from buyers to sellers (the b and c triangles). This happens because the availability of new substitutes for the product depicted in figure 1 will usually make competition denser and, hence, more intense. Rare is the case where new substitutes do not increase the elasticity of D.[6]

Several of these insights from figure 1 simultaneously feature efficiency gains and distributional shifts from sellers to buyers that many people welcome. Such happy combinations of efficiency and equity gains are not always the rule, however. Two further insights from figure 1 feature trade-offs between efficiency gains and redistribution from powerful sellers to (weak) buyers. One concerns price discrimination, the other, innovation.

---

4. Thus, members of the European Union are jointly opening formerly monopolized telecommunications markets to other EU suppliers on 1 January 1998.

5. See, for first-pass calculations, Hufbauer (1996).

6. The technical point being described is summarized by the Euler-equation constraints on elasticities: the sum of the (negative) own-price elasticity plus both the (usually positive) income elasticity and all the cross-price elasticities with respect to substitutes (positive) or complements (negative) must equal zero. When a new substitute becomes available and a new positive term is therefore added to the cross-price elasticities, then some other element in the summation must become more negative (or less positive) to compensate. For the income elasticity to become less psoitive seems unlikely, as does the special case where the entire impact of a new positive cross-price elasticity is absorbed by adjustments in the values of other cross-price elasticities. Far more likely, and far more intuitive, is for the own-price elasticity to grow somewhat more negative when a new close substitute appears. Demand becomes more elastic when there are more altrenative products.

Under price discrimination and for entirely new products and innovations, the various triangles and rectangles in figure 1 change shape and interpretation.

Price discrimination describes a situation where sellers can extend their price-setting market power to isolate buyers from each other. Then they can charge different prices to different isolated buyers—in the extreme, all that each buyer can bear. In this extreme for figure 1, we could interpret the demand curve as a rank ordering of specific buyers from left to right, with the most desperate at the left, the second-most-desperate adjacent to him/her, and the least desperate buyer on the right. Desperation can be readily measured by the maximum price that a buyer is willing to pay for the product rather than doing without.[7] When a firm has the power to isolate buyers from each other, it can charge each buyer the maximum they can bear and essentially extract the entirety of the buyers (consumer) surplus for its own pocket. Under this extreme (perfect) price discrimination, the triangles a_1 and a_2 become part of the surplus captured by the powerful seller, a surplus (profit) additional to that represented by the boxes b_1 and b_2.

With barriers to entry, price-discriminating firms are arguably more profitable than comparable firms that cannot discriminate, and their additional profits (surplus) come at the expense of buyers, who are, in the extreme, left with no surplus at all. Many people find this unfair, which is why competition policies try to discipline the practice.

In more general types of price discrimination, there are additional possibilities for welfare effects. Figure 1 may be, in essence, carved up into pieces, representing segmented submarkets. There is no guarantee that the sum of the quantities supplied in the submarkets will exceed Q_1; when it falls short, market power has been enhanced and the efficiency loss represented by areas c_1 and c_2 may grow. Price-discriminating power will have enhanced price-setting power. If the additional profits from price discrimination enhance entry, however, these efficiency losses are less likely.[8]

In global markets, moreover, there may be a unique kind of welfare loss as well. Where the seller is a foreign firm, then the transfer of areas a_1 and a_2 from buyers to producer(s) is also a national welfare (efficiency) loss—another form of beggar-thy-neighbor rent shifting. This is what makes cross-border price discrimination potentially different than price discrimination within a country and what, therefore, provides a possible defense of antidumping trade remedies from the perspective of

---

7. That is, technically, the buyer's reservation price.

8. And even when entry is disregarded, price discrimination can pay an efficiency bonus if it becomes the instrument by which implicitly-colluding oligopolists cheat on each other.

competition policies, even when those policies do not necessarily pros-
ecute the same practice domestically.[9]

But there are two cautions against leaping too quickly toward policy
discipline for price discrimination and antidumping border measures.
(After all, price discrimination is a murky area, as the text suggests.)
One caution is that there may be an efficiency gain to trade off against
any inequities. This is easily seen in the extreme of perfect price discrimination. There, the monopolistic firm's marginal revenue curve is
not MR; the relevant marginal revenue curve actually coincides with D.
This occurs because the firm extracts the maximum price/revenue from
its most desperate customer, then does the same to its second-most-
desperate, and so on through all its customers, without being forced to
sacrifice revenue on the inframarginal units as a single-price monopolist
must. The point of equality between marginal revenue (D, in this case)
and marginal cost (MC) is D^*, exactly the same as the perfectly competitive equilibrium. Therefore, deadweight loss is eliminated and perfect
price discrimination drives out inefficiency.

The second caution is that price discrimination may actually advance a
slightly different conception of equity! Price discrimination can make it
worthwhile (i.e., profitable) for a firm to sell to less desperate customers—
those to the right on the (rank-ordered) D curve who would otherwise
have been priced out of the market for the illustrated good. Thus, price
discrimination may increase product availability and pull in buyers who
are otherwise discriminated against by unavailability. Desperate buyers—
those willing to pay high prices—bear the burden of such redistribution.
Because it is often the rich who will pay anything for a good rather than
do without it, and the poor who are priced out of markets by monopolistic
market power, price discrimination can often end up being an indirect
device for redistributing from rich to poor buyers.[10]

Innovation can also involve an efficiency-equity trade-off for competition policies that can be seen in figure 1. If it is correct (as often argued)

9. In the more general types of price discrimination, the efficiency argument must take
into account two further social costs of price discrimination. One is that the barriers that
firms themselves often set up to isolate buyers (so-called hurdles, such as clipping a
coupon to bring to the grocery store) often involve a resource sacrifice (e.g., clipping
time, extra trips to the store), as do the firm's costs of advertising the hurdles and of
acquiring the inforamtion necessary to rank its various customers by degree of desperation. A second cost is that price-discriminating firms often enlist government regulations
that help isolate their customers from each other (for example, no one but the big North
American automakers can trade autos freely between the Unite States and Canada), and
these regulations impose unique efficiency costs and inequities that would vanish if price
discrimination incentives disappeared.

10. Remembering, however, that the owners of the firms, often the rich themselves, are
the ones who redistribute surplus through price discrimination, from all buyers, rich and
poor!

that innovations are not profitable unless some monopolistic property right (patents, industrial secrets, etc.) to them is granted, then the appropriate comparisons and interpretations in figure 1 change again. Let the diagram now describe quantities produced (Q) of some very specific innovation that requires a fixed outlay of up-front resources for research. Point D^* (perfect competition) is not feasible (because it is unprofitable). Monopolistic D_1 is barely feasible, let us assume, because the b_1 and b_2 just finances the fixed research resources. Everything between D^* and D_1 yields some profit, but not enough to finance the innovation (by assumption). So the only other equilibriums lie trivially above D_1, where none of the innovation is produced. The interpretation of areas a_1, a_2, b_1, b_2 does not change much; they are the surplus—welfare gain—from the innovation. But triangular areas c_1 and c_2 are no longer a welfare (deadweight) loss, since D^* was never a feasible equilibrium.[11] In policy terms, monopoly is the desirable policy on efficiency grounds for delivering the gains (a_1 or a_2 plus b_1 or b_2) from this particular innovation. And it may be efficient and fair for the monopolistic owner of the innovation property right to be able to price discriminate if and when it is to be sold—which is exactly what a system of negotiated licenses is, each with its own fee (price) dependent on the desperation of the potential licensee.

From this point of view, competition policies should be less strict for innovative products and processes.[12] Efficiency losses are smaller and price discrimination is fairer than for other products and processes. And monopolistic property rights, including industrial secrets, should be protected on a marketwide—often global-basis.[13] But full efficiency, much less equality, is impossible, because monopoly of fixed length and with rigid other terms is never the perfect innovation-enhancing policy. So distortions remain. Traditional antidumping policies are among the most important, which, in the case of innovation, may distort efficient collection of the appropriate reward by the innovator. The innovator's appropriate reward includes the reward from price discrimination (unlike the case of garden-variety goods described above) (see Katz and Ordover 1990).

Finally, figure 1 is a mere one-period snapshot. Its equilibriums will change if current pricing and other nonprice decisions (quality, location, etc.) affect future market prospects, especially entry by potential rivals. Thus, for example, a real monopolist might choose a price below P_1, a quantity above Q_1, and a more suitable quality to deter the entry of a

---

11. Neither were any points between D* and D1.

12. See Jorde and Teece (1992) for extensive argument to this effect. See Scherer and Ross (1990, chapter 17) for a more skeptical view and summary of the evidence.

13. As is done in the recent Uruguay Round agreement on TRIPS.

second competitor that would force the monopolist to P_2, Q_2 (the duopolistic equilibrium) in the future. The monopolist would see that an indefinite sequence of profits that were somewhat smaller than box b_1 would be better than a sequence of temporary, full series of b1 followed by that of b_2 forever after.

Policies that facilitate free trade and free entry invite the benefits of this kind of favorable entry deterrence (consumer surplus is higher and unfair excess profits are lower than for full monopoly). Both types of policies enhance contestability.

References

Besanko, David, David Dranove, and Mark Shanley. 1996. *The Economics of Strategy*. New York: John Wiley.

Bhagwati, Jagdish N., and Robert E. Hudec, eds. 1996. *Fair Trade and Harmonization: Prerequisites for Free Trade?* Cambridge: MIT Press.

Bond, Eric. 1996. A "Natural Experiment" Using State Level Antitrust Policies. University Park: Pennsylvania State University. Photocopy.

Bourgeois, Jacques H. J., and Patrick A. Messerlin. 1993. Competition and the EC Antidumping Regulation. Manuscript. Paris: Institut d'Études Politique de Paris.

Bresnahan, Timothy F. 1989. Empirical Studies of Industries with Market Power. In *The Handbook of Industrial Organization*, ed. by Richard Schmalensee and Robert Willig. Amsterdam: North Holland.

Bresnahan, Timothy F., and Peter C. Reiss. 1991. Entry and Competition in Concentrated Markets. *Journal of Political Economy* 99, no. 5 (October): 977-1009.

Cho, Soon. 1994. *The Dynamics of Korean Economic Development*. Washington: Institute for International Economics.

Commission of the European Communities. 1997. Green Paper on Vertical Restraints in EC Competition Policy. Brussels: Commission of the European Communities (22 January).

Dick, Andrew. 1997. When Are Cartels Stable Contracts? *Journal of Law and Economics* 39 (April 1996): 241-83.

Dinopoulos, Elias. 1994. Schumpeterian Growth Theory: An Overview. *Osaka City University Economic Review* 29: 1-21.

Eminent Persons Group (EPG). 1995. *Implementing the APEC Vision: Third Report of the Eminent Persons Group*. Singapore: APEC Secretariat (August).

Feketekuty, Geza, and Robert A. Rogowsky. 1996. The Scope, Implication and Economic Rationale of a Competition-Oriented Approach to Future Multilateral Trade Negotiations. Manuscript. Monterey, CA: Monterey Institute of International Studies (May).

Finger, J. Michael. 1995. Can Dispute Settlement Contribute to an International Agreement (Institutional Order) on Locational Competition? In *Locational Competition in* the World Economy: Symposium 1994, ed. by Horst Siebert. Tubingen, Germany: J. C. B. Mohr (Paul Siebeck).

First, Harry, Eleanor M. Fox, and Robert Pitofsky, eds. 1991. *Revitalizing Antitrust in Its Second Century: Essays on Legal, Economic, and Political Policy.* New York: Quorum.

Fox, Eleanor M. 1997a. US and EU Competition Law: A Comparison. In *Global Competition Policy,* ed. by Edward M. Graham and J. David Richardson. Washington: Institute for International Economics.

Fox, Eleanor M. 1997b. Toward World Antitrust and Market Access. *The American Journal of International Law* 91, no. 1 (January).

Fox, Eleanor M., and Janusz A. Ordover. 1995. The Harmonization of Competition and Trade Law—The Case for Modest Linkages of Law and Limits to Parochial State Action. *World Competition* 19 (December): 5-34.

Geroski, P. A. 1992. Vertical Relations between Firms and Industrial Policy. *The Economic Journal* 102, no. 410 (January): 138-47.

Gifford, Daniel J. 1997. The Draft International Antitrust Code Proposed at Munich: Good Intentions Gone Awry. *Minnesota Journal of Global Trade* 6, no. 1: 1-66.

Gifford, Daniel J., and Mitsuo Matsushita. 1996. Antitrust or Competition Laws Viewed in a Trading Context: Harmony or Dissonance? In *Fair Trade and Harmonization: Prerequisites for Free Trade?* ed. by Jagdish N. Bhagwati and Robert E. Hudec. Cambridge: MIT Press.

Goldman, Calvin S., John D. Bodrug, and Mark A. Warner. 1997. Canada. In *Global Competition Policy,* ed. by Edward M. Graham and J. David Richardson. Washington: Institute for International Economics.

Graham, Edward M. 1994. US Antitrust Laws and Market Access to Japan. In *Unilateral Application of Antitrust and Trade Laws,* ed. by Henry B. Cortesi. New York: The Pacific Institute/The Asia Institute.

Graham, Edward M. 1995. Competition Policy and the New Trade Agenda. In *New Dimensions of Market Access in a Globalizing World Economy.* OECD Documents. Paris: Organization for Economic Cooperation and Development.

Graham, Edward M. 1996a. *Global Corporations and National Governments.* Washington: Institute for International Economics.

Graham, Edward M. 1996b. Competition Policy in the United States. In *Competition Regulation in the Pacific Rim,* ed. by Carl. J. Green and Douglas E. Rosenthal. New York: Oceana Press.

Graham, Edward M., and Robert Z. Lawrence. 1996. Measuring the International Contestability of Markets: A Conceptual Approach. *Journal of World Trade* 30, no. 5, (October): 5-20.

Graham, Edward M., and J. David Richardson, eds. 1997. *Global Competition Policy.* Washington: Institute for International Economics.

Graham, Edward M., and Christopher Wilkie. 1994. Multinationals and the Investment Provisions of the NAFTA. *The International Trade Journal* 8, no. 3 (Spring).

Greaney, Theresa M. 1996. Import Now! An Analysis of Market-Share Voluntary Import Expansions (VIEs). *Journal of International Economics* 40, no. 1/2 (February): 149-63.

Green, Carl J., and Douglas E. Rosenthal, eds. 1996. *Competition Regulation Within the APEC Region: Commonality and Divergence.* New York: Oceana Press.

Greenhut, Melvin L., George Norman, and Chao-shun Hung. 1987. *The Economics of Imperfect Competition: A Spatial Approach.* Cambridge: Cambridge University Press.

Gual, Jordi. 1995. *The Coherence of EC Policies on Trade, Competition and Industry.* Discussion Paper No. 1105. London: Centre for Economic Policy Research (January).

Hay, Donald. 1997. United Kingdom. In *Global Competition Policy,* ed. by Edward M. Graham and J. David Richardson. Washington: Institute for International Economics.

Hindley, Brian. 1996. Competition Law and the WTO: Alternative Structures for Agreement. In *Fair Trade and Harmonization: Prerequisites for Free Trade?* ed. by Jagdish N. Bhagwati and Robert E. Hudec. Cambridge: MIT Press.

Hoekman, Bernard. 1996. *Trade and Competition Policy in the WTO System.* CEPR Discussion Paper No. 1501. London: Centre for Economic Policy and Research.

Hoekman, Bernard. 1997a. Focal Points and Multilateral Negotiations on the Contestability of Markets. In *Quiet Pioneering: Robert M. Stern and His International Economic Legacy,* ed. by Keith E. Maskus, et al. Ann Arbor: University of Michigan Press. Forthcoming.

Hoekman, Bernard. 1997b. Competition Policy and the Global Trading System. *The World Economy* 20 (July): 383-406.

Hoekman, Bernard M., and Petros C. Mavroidis. 1994. Competition, Competition Policy, and the GATT. *The World Economy* 17, no. 2 (March): 121-50.

Horn, Henrik, and James Levinsohn. 1997. *Merger Policies and Trade Liberalization.* National Bureau of Economic Research Working Paper No. 6077 (June): National Bureau of Economic Research.

Hufbauer, Gary. 1996. Surveying the Costs of Protection: A Partial Equilibrium Approach. In *The World Trading System: Challenges Ahead,* ed. by Jeffrey J. Schott. Washington: Institute for International Economics.

Irmen, Andreas, and Jacques-Francois Thisse. 1996. Competition in Multi-Characteristics Spaces: Hotelling Was Almost Right. Centre for Economic Policy Research Discussion Paper no. 1446 (October). London: Centre for Economic Policy.

Itoh, Motoshige, and Sadao Nagaoka. 1997. VERs, VIEs, and Global Competition. In *Global Competition Policy,* ed. by Edward M. Graham and J. David Richardson. Washington: Institute for International Economics.

Jackson, John H. 1990. *Restructuring the GATT System.* New York: Council on Foreign Relations Press for the Royal Institute of International Affairs.

Jenny, Frédéric. 1997. France. In *Global Competition Policy,* ed. by Edward M. Graham and J. David Richardson. Washington: Institute for International Economics.

Joelson, Mark R. 1993. Antitrust Aspects of NAFTA. *Federal Bar News & Journal* 40, no. 9 (October): 573-78.

Jorde, Thomas M., and David J. Teece, eds. 1992. *Antitrust, Innovation, and Competitiveness.* New York: Oxford University Press.

Katz, Michael L., and Janusz A. Ordover. 1990. R&D Cooperation and Competition. *Brookings Papers on Economic Activity: Microeconomics, 1990*: 137-91.

Kühn, Kai Uwe. 1997. Germany. In *Global Competition Policy,* ed. by Edward M. Graham and J. David Richardson. Washington: Institute for International Economics.

Kühn, Kai-Uwe, Paul Seabright, and Alasdair Smith. 1992. *Competition Policy Research: Where Do We Stand?* CEPR Occasional Paper No. 8. London: Centre for Economic Policy and Research (July).

Lawrence, Robert Z., Albert Bressand, and Takatoshi Ito. 1996. *A Vision for the World Economy: Openness, Diversity, and Cohesion.* Washington: Brookings Institution.

Levinsohn, James. 1996. Competition Policy and International Trade. In *Fair Trade and Harmonization: Prerequisites for Free Trade?* ed. by Jagdish N. Bhagwati and Robert E. Hudec. Cambridge: MIT Press.

Lipstein, Robert A. 1997. Using Antitrust Principles to Reform Antidumping Law. In *Global Competition Policy,* ed. by Edward M. Graham and J. David Richardson. Washington: Institute for International Economics.

Lloyd, Peter, and Gary Sampson. 1995. Competition and Trade Policy: Identifying the Issues after the Uruguay Round. *World Economy* 18, no. 5 (September): 681-705.

Malueg, David A. 1993. Bounding the Welfare Effects of Third Degree Price Discrimination. *American Economic Review* 83 (September): 1011-21.

Malueg, David A., and Marius Schwartz. 1994. Parallel Imports, Demand Dispersion, and International Price Discrimination *Journal of International Economics* 37: 167-95.

Mathewson, Frank, Michael Trebilcock, and Michael Walker, eds. 1990. *The Law and Economics of Competition Policy.* Vancouver: Fraser Institute.

Matsushita, Mitsuo. 1997. Japan. In *Global Competition Policy,* ed. by Edward M. Graham and J. David Richardson. Washington: Institute for International Economics.

Messerlin, Patrick A. 1996. Competition Policy and Antidumping Reform: An Exercise in Transition. In *The World Trading System: Challenges Ahead,* ed. by Jeffrey J. Schott. Washington: Institute for International Economics.

Neven, Damien, Robin Nuttall, and Paul Seabright. 1993. *Merger in Daylight: The Economics and Politics of European Merger Control.* London: Centre for Economic Policy Research.

Noland, Marcus. 1997. Host-Country Market Structure and Inward FDI. Photocopy. Washington: Institute for International Economics.

Ordover, Janusz A. 1990. Economic Foundations of Competition Policy. In *Competition Policy in Europe and North America: Economic Issues and Institutions,* ed. by W. S. Comanor et al. Chur, Switerland: Harwood.

Organization for Economic Cooperation and Development (OECD). 1989. *Predatory Pricing.* Paris: Organization for Economic Cooperation and Development.

Peck, Merton J., Richard C. Levin, and Akira Goto. 1988. Picking Losers: Public Policy Toward Declining Industries in Japan In *Government Policy Toward Industry in the United States and Japan,* ed. by John B. Shoven. Cambridge, UK: Cambridge University Press.

Richardson, J. David. 1995. Comment on Can Dispute Settlement Contribute to an International Agreement (Institutional Order) on Locational Competition? (by J. Michael Finger). In *Locational Competition in the World Economy: Symposium 1994,* ed. by Horst Siebert. Tubingen, Germany: J. C. B. Mohr (Paul Siebeck).

Richardson, J. David. 1997. Competition Policies as Irritants to Asia-Pacific Trade. In *East Asian Trade After the Uruguay Round,* ed. by David Robertson. New York: Cambridge University Press.

Rosenthal, Douglas E., and Mitsuo Matsushita. 1997. Competition in Japan and the West: Can the Approaches Be Reconciled? In *Global Competition Policy,* ed. by Edward M. Graham and J. David Richardson. Washington: Institute for International Economics.

Rosenthal, Douglas E., and Phedon Nicholaides. 1997. Harmonizing Antitrust: The Less Effective Way to Promote International Competition. In *Global Competition Policy,* ed. by Edward M. Graham and J. David Richardson. Washington: Institute for International Economics.

Scherer, F. M. 1992. *International High-Technology Competition.* Cambridge: Harvard University Press.

Scherer, F. M. 1994. *Competition Policies for an Integrated World Economy.* Washington: Brookings Institution.

Scherer, F. M., and David Ross. 1980. *Industrial Market Structure and Economic Performance.* 2nd ed. Boston: Houghton Mifflin.

Scherer, F. M., and David Ross. 1990. *Industrial Market Structure and Economic Performance.* 3d ed. Boston: Houghton Mifflin.

Schott, Jeffrey J., ed. 1996. *The World Trading System: Challenges Ahead.* Washington: Institute for International Economics.

Schumpeter, Joseph. 1950. *Capitalism, Socialism, and Democracy.* New York: Harper Collins.

Shaw, R. W., and S. A. Shaw. 1983. Excess Capacity and Rationalization in the Western European Synthetic Fibres Industry. *The Journal of Industrial Economics* 32 (December): 149-66.

Sheard, Paul. 1997. *Keiretsu,* Competition, and Market Access. In *Global Competition Policy,* ed. by Edward M. Graham and J. David Richardson. Washington: Institute for International Economics.

Shin, Hyun Ja. 1992. Census and Analysis of Antidumping Cases in the United States. Monograph. NJ: Princeton University.

Smith, P. J. 1997. Are Weak Patent Rights a Barrier to U.S. Exports? Photocopy (31 May).

Suzumura, Kotaro. 1997. Formal and Informal Measures for Controlling Competition in Japan: Institutional Overview and Theoretical Evaluation. In *Global Competition Policy,* ed. by Edward M. Graham and J. David Richardson. Washington: Institute for International Economics.

Thomson, Graeme. 1997. Australia and New Zealand. In *Global Competition Policy*, ed. by Edward M. Graham and J. David Richardson. Washington: Institute for International Economics.

Tineo, Luis. 1997. *Competition Policy and Law in Latin America: From Distributive Regulations to Market Efficiency*. Center for Trade and Commercial Diplomacy Working Paper No. 4. Monterey, CA: Monterey Institute of International Studies.

Tybout, James R., and M. Daniel Westbrook. 1995. Trade Liberalization and the Dimensions of Efficiency Change in Mexican Manufacturing Industries. *Journal of International Economics* 39: 53-78.

UNCTAD (United Nations Conference on Trade and Development). 1997. *World Investment Report 1997: Transnational Corporations, Market Structure, and Competition Policy*. New York and Geneva.

Varian, Hal R. 1989. Price Discrimination. In *Handbook of Industrial Organization*, vol. 1, ed. by Richard Schmalansee and Robert Willig. Amsterdam: North Holland.

Vernon, Raymond, and Kalypso Nicolaïdis. 1997. European Union. In *Global Competition Policy*, ed. by Edward M. Graham and J. David Richardson. Washington: Institute for International Economics.

Other Publications from the
Institute for International Economics

POLICY ANALYSES IN INTERNATIONAL ECONOMICS Series

1   **The Lending Policies of the International Monetary Fund**
    John Williamson/*August 1982*
                             ISBN paper 0-88132-000-5   72 pp.

2   **"Reciprocity": A New Approach to World Trade Policy?**
    William R. Cline/*September 1982*
                             ISBN paper 0-88132-001-3   41 pp.

3   **Trade Policy in the 1980s**
    C. Fred Bergsten and William R. Cline/*November 1982*
    (out of print)   ISBN paper 0-88132-002-1   84 pp.
    Partially reproduced in the book *Trade Policy in the 1980s*.

4   **International Debt and the Stability of the World Economy**
    William R. Cline/*September 1983*
                             ISBN paper 0-88132-010-2   134 pp.

5   **The Exchange Rate System,** Second Edition
    John Williamson/*September 1983, rev. June 1985*
    (out of print)   ISBN paper 0-88132-034-X   61 pp.

6   **Economic Sanctions in Support of Foreign Policy Goals**
    Gary Clyde Hufbauer and Jeffrey J. Schott/*October 1983*
                             ISBN paper 0-88132-014-5   109 pp.

7   **A New SDR Allocation?**
    John Williamson/*March 1984*
                             ISBN paper 0-88132-028-5   61 pp.

8   **An International Standard for Monetary Stabilization**
    Ronald I. McKinnon/*March 1984*
    (out of print)   ISBN paper 0-88132-018-8   108 pp.

9   **The Yen/Dollar Agreement: Liberalizing Japanese Capital Markets**
    Jeffrey A. Frankel/*December 1984*
                             ISBN paper 0-88132-035-8   86 pp.

10 **Bank Lending to Developing Countries: The Policy Alternatives**
    C. Fred Bergsten, William R. Cline, and John Williamson/*April 1985*
                             ISBN paper 0-88132-032-3   221 pp.

11 **Trading for Growth: The Next Round of Trade Negotiations**
    Gary Clyde Hufbauer and Jeffrey J. Schott/*September 1985*
    (out of print)   ISBN paper 0-88132-033-1   109 pp.

12 **Financial Intermediation Beyond the Debt Crisis**
    Donald R. Lessard and John Williamson/*September 1985*
    (out of print)   ISBN paper 0-88132-021-8   130 pp.

13 **The United States-Japan Economic Problem**
    C. Fred Bergsten and William R. Cline/*October 1985, 2d ed. January 1987*
    (out of print)   ISBN paper 0-88132-060-9   180 pp.

14 **Deficits and the Dollar: The World Economy at Risk**
    Stephen Marris/*December 1985, 2d ed. November 1987*
    (out of print)   ISBN paper 0-88132-067-6   415 pp.

15 **Trade Policy for Troubled Industries**
    Gary Clyde Hufbauer and Howard F. Rosen/*March 1986*
                             ISBN paper 0-88132-020-X   111 pp.

16 **The United States and Canada: The Quest for Free Trade**
    Paul Wonnacott, with an Appendix by John Williamson/*March 1987*
                             ISBN paper 0-88132-056-0   188 pp.

BOOKS

Trade Policy in the 1980s
William R. Cline, editor/*1983*
(out of print)   ISBN paper 0-88132-031-5   810 pp.

Subsidies in International Trade
Gary Clyde Hufbauer and Joanna Shelton Erb/*1984*
          ISBN cloth 0-88132-004-8   299 pp.

International Debt: Systemic Risk and Policy Response
William R. Cline/*1984*   ISBN cloth 0-88132-015-3   336 pp.

Trade Protection in the United States: 31 Case Studies
Gary Clyde Hufbauer, Diane E. Berliner, and Kimberly Ann Elliott/*1986*
(out of print)   ISBN paper 0-88132-040-4   371 pp.

Toward Renewed Economic Growth in Latin America
Bela Balassa, Gerardo M. Bueno, Pedro-Pablo Kuczynski,
and Mario Henrique Simonsen/*1986*
(out of stock)   ISBN paper 0-88132-045-5   205 pp.

Capital Flight and Third World Debt
Donald R. Lessard and John Williamson, editors/*1987*
(out of print)   ISBN paper 0-88132-053-6   270 pp.

The Canada-United States Free Trade Agreement: The Global Impact
Jeffrey J. Schott and Murray G. Smith, editors/*1988*
          ISBN paper 0-88132-073-0   211 pp.

World Agricultural Trade: Building a Consensus
William M. Miner and Dale E. Hathaway, editors/*1988*
          ISBN paper 0-88132-071-3   226 pp.

Japan in the World Economy
Bela Balassa and Marcus Noland/*1988*
          ISBN paper 0-88132-041-2   306 pp.

America in the World Economy: A Strategy for the 1990s
C. Fred Bergsten/*1988*   ISBN cloth 0-88132-089-7   235 pp.
          ISBN paper 0-88132-082-X   235 pp.

Managing the Dollar: From the Plaza to the Louvre
Yoichi Funabashi/*1988, 2d ed. 1989*
          ISBN paper 0-88132-097-8   307 pp.

United States External Adjustment and the World Economy
William R. Cline/*May 1989*   ISBN paper 0-88132-048-X   392 pp.

Free Trade Areas and U.S. Trade Policy
Jeffrey J. Schott, editor/*May 1989*
          ISBN paper 0-88132-094-3   400 pp.

Dollar Politics: Exchange Rate Policymaking in the United States
I. M. Destler and C. Randall Henning/*September 1989*
(out of print)   ISBN paper 0-88132-079-X   192 pp.

Latin American Adjustment: How Much Has Happened?
John Williamson, editor/*April 1990*
          ISBN paper 0-88132-125-7   480 pp.

The Future of World Trade in Textiles and Apparel
William R. Cline/*1987, 2d ed. June 1990*
          ISBN paper 0-88132-110-9   344 pp.

**Completing the Uruguay Round: A Results-Oriented Approach
to the GATT Trade Negotiations**
Jeffrey J. Schott, editor/*September 1990*
          ISBN paper 0-88132-130-3   256 pp.

Economic Sanctions Reconsidered (in two volumes)
Economic Sanctions Reconsidered: Supplemental Case Histories
Gary Clyde Hufbauer, Jeffrey J. Schott, and Kimberly Ann Elliott/*1985, 2d ed. December 1990*
          ISBN cloth 0-88132-115-X   928 pp.
          ISBN paper 0-88132-105-2   928 pp.

Economic Sanctions Reconsidered: History and Current Policy
Gary Clyde Hufbauer, Jeffrey J. Schott, and Kimberly Ann Elliott/*December 1990*
                                ISBN cloth 0-88132-136-2   288 pp.
                                ISBN paper 0-88132-140-0   288 pp.

Pacific Basin Developing Countries: Prospects for the Future
Marcus Noland/*January 1991*   ISBN   cloth 0-88132-141-9   250 pp.
(out of print)   ISBN paper 0-88132-081-1   250 pp.

Currency Convertibility in Eastern Europe
John Williamson, editor/*October 1991*
                                ISBN paper 0-88132-128-1   396 pp.

International Adjustment and Financing: The Lessons of 1985-1991
C. Fred Bergsten, editor/*January 1992*
                                ISBN paper 0-88132-112-5   336 pp.

North American Free Trade: Issues and Recommendations
Gary Clyde Hufbauer and Jeffrey J. Schott/*April 1992*
                                ISBN paper 0-88132-120-6   392 pp.

Narrowing the U.S. Current Account Deficit
Allen J. Lenz/*June 1992*
(out of print)   ISBN paper 0-88132-103-6   640 pp.

The Economics of Global Warming
William R. Cline/*June 1992*   ISBN paper 0-88132-132-X   416 pp.

U.S. Taxation of International Income: Blueprint for Reform
Gary Clyde Hufbauer, assisted by Joanna M. van Rooij/*October 1992*
                                ISBN cloth 0-88132-178-8   304 pp.
                                ISBN paper 0-88132-134-6   304 pp.

Who's Bashing Whom? Trade Conflict in High-Technology Industries
Laura D'Andrea Tyson/*November 1992*
                                ISBN paper 0-88132-106-0   352 pp.

Korea in the World Economy
Il SaKong/*January 1993*   ISBN paper 0-88132-106-0   328 pp.

Pacific Dynamism and the International Economic System
C. Fred Bergsten and Marcus Noland, editors/*May 1993*
                                ISBN paper 0-88132-196-6   424 pp.

Economic Consequences of Soviet Disintegration
John Williamson, editor/*May 1993*
                                ISBN paper 0-88132-190-7   664 pp.

Reconcilable Differences? United States-Japan Economic Conflict
C. Fred Bergsten and Marcus Noland/*June 1993*
                                ISBN paper 0-88132-129-X   296 pp.

Does Foreign Exchange Intervention Work?
Kathryn M. Dominguez and Jeffrey A. Frankel/*September 1993*
                                ISBN paper 0-88132-104-4   192 pp.

Sizing Up U.S. Export Disincentives
J. David Richardson/*September 1993*
                                ISBN paper 0-88132-107-9   192 pp.

NAFTA: An Assessment
Gary Clyde Hufbauer and Jeffrey J. Schott/*rev. ed. October 1993*
                                ISBN paper 0-88132-199-0   216 pp.

Adjusting to Volatile Energy Prices
Philip K. Verleger, Jr./*November 1993*
                                ISBN paper 0-88132-069-2   288 pp.

The Political Economy of Policy Reform
John Williamson, editor/*January 1994*
                                ISBN paper 0-88132-195-8   624 pp.

Measuring the Costs of Protection in the United States
Gary Clyde Hufbauer and Kimberly Ann Elliott/*January 1994*
                                ISBN paper 0-88132-108-7   144 pp.
The Dynamics of Korean Economic Development
Cho Soon/*March 1994*
                                ISBN paper 0-88132-162-1   272 pp.

Reviving the European Union
C. Randall Henning, Eduard Hochreiter and Gary Clyde Hufbauer, editors/*April 1994*
ISBN paper 0-88132-208-3   192 pp.

China in the World Economy
Nicholas R. Lardy/*April 1994*
ISBN paper 0-88132-200-8   176 pp.

Greening the GATT: Trade, Environment, and the Future
Daniel C. Esty/*July 1994*
ISBN paper 0-88132-205-9   344 pp.

Western Hemisphere Economic Integration
Gary Clyde Hufbauer and Jeffrey J. Schott/*July 1994*
ISBN paper 0-88132-159-1   304 pp.

Currencies and Politics in the United States, Germany, and Japan
C. Randall Henning/*September 1994*
ISBN paper 0-88132-127-3   432 pp.

Estimating Equilibrium Exchange Rates
John Williamson, editor/*September 1994*
ISBN paper 0-88132-076-5   320 pp.

Managing the World Economy: Fifty Years After Bretton Woods
Peter B. Kenen, editor/*September 1994*
ISBN paper 0-88132-212-1   448 pp.

Reciprocity and Retaliation in U.S. Trade Policy
Thomas O. Bayard and Kimberly Ann Elliott/*September 1994*
ISBN paper 0-88132-084-6   528 pp.

The Uruguay Round: An Assessment
Jeffrey J. Schott, assisted by Johanna W. Buurman/*November 1994*
ISBN paper 0-88132-206-7   240 pp.

Measuring the Costs of Protection in Japan
Yoko Sazanami, Shujiro Urata, and Hiroki Kawai/*January 1995*
ISBN paper 0-88132-211-3   96 pp.

Foreign Direct Investment in the United States, Third Edition
Edward M. Graham and Paul R. Krugman/*January 1995*
ISBN paper 0-88132-204-0   232 pp.

The Political Economy of Korea-United States Cooperation
C. Fred Bergsten and Il SaKong, editors/*February 1995*
ISBN paper 0-88132-213-X   128 pp.

International Debt Reexamined
William R. Cline/*February 1995*
ISBN paper 0-88132-083-8   560 pp.

American Trade Politics, Third Edition
I. M. Destler/*April 1995*   ISBN paper 0-88132-215-6   360 pp.

Managing Official Export Credits: The Quest for a Global Regime
John E. Ray/*July 1995*   ISBN paper 0-88132-207-5   344 pp.

Asia Pacific Fusion: Japan's Role in APEC
Yoichi Funabashi/*October 1995*
ISBN paper 0-88132-224-5   312 pp.

Korea-United States Cooperation in the New World Order
C. Fred Bergsten and Il SaKong, editors/*February 1996*
ISBN paper 0-88132-226-1   144 pp.

Why Exports Really Matter!   ISBN paper 0-88132-221-0   34 pp.
Why Exports Matter More!   ISBN paper 0-88132-229-6   36 pp.
J. David Richardson and Karin Rindal/*July 1995; February 1996*

Global Corporations and National Governments
Edward M. Graham/*May 1996*
ISBN paper 0-88132-111-7   168 pp.

Global Economic Leadership and the Group of Seven
C. Fred Bergsten and C. Randall Henning/*May 1996*
ISBN paper 0-88132-218-0   192 pp.

The Trading System After the Uruguay Round
John Whalley and Colleen Hamilton/*July 1996*
ISBN paper 0-88132-131-1
224 pp.

Private Capital Flows to Emerging Markets After the Mexican Crisis
Guillermo A. Calvo, Morris Goldstein, and Eduard Hochreiter/*September 1996*
ISBN paper 0-88132-232-6
352 pp.

The Crawling Band as an Exchange Rate Regime:
Lessons from Chile, Colombia, and Israel
John Williamson/*September 1996*
ISBN paper 0-88132-231-8
192 pp.

Flying High: Civil Aviation in the Asia Pacific
Gary Clyde Hufbauer and Christopher Findlay/*November 1996*
ISBN paper 0-88132-231-8
232 pp.

Measuring the Costs of Visible Protection in Korea
Namdoo Kim/*November 1996*
ISBN paper 0-88132-236-9
112 pp.

The World Trading System: Challenges Ahead
Jeffrey J. Schott/*December 1996*
ISBN paper 0-88132-235-0
350 pp.

Has Globalization Gone Too Far?
Dani Rodrik/*March 1997*   ISBN cloth 0-88132-243-1
128 pp.

Korea-United States Economic Relationship
C. Fred Bergsten and Il SaKong, editors/*March 1997*
ISBN paper 0-88132-240-7
152 pp.

Summitry in the Americas: A Progress Report
Richard E. Feinberg/*April 1997*
ISBN paper 0-88132-242-3
272 pp.

Corruption and the Global Economy
Kimberly Ann Elliott/*June 1997*
ISBN paper 0-88132-233-4
256 pp.

Regional Trading Blocs in the World Economic System
Jeffrey A. Frankel/*October 1997*
ISBN paper 0-88132-202-4
346 pp.

Sustaining the Asia Pacific Miracle: Environmental Protection and
Economic Integration
André Dua and Daniel C. Esty/*October 1997*
ISBN paper 0-88132-250-4
232 pp.

Trade and Income Distribution
William R. Cline/*November1997*
ISBN paper 0-88132-216-4
296 pp.

SPECIAL REPORTS

1 **Promoting World Recovery: A Statement on Global Economic Strategy**
   by Twenty-six Economists from Fourteen Countries/*December 1982*
   (out of print)   ISBN paper 0-88132-013-7
45 pp.

2 **Prospects for Adjustment in Argentina, Brazil, and Mexico:**
   Responding to the Debt Crisis   (out of print)
   John Williamson, editor/*June 1983*
ISBN paper 0-88132-016-1
71 pp.

3 **Inflation and Indexation: Argentina, Brazil, and Israel**
   John Williamson, editor/*March 1985*
ISBN paper 0-88132-037-4
191 pp.

4 **Global Economic Imbalances**
   C. Fred Bergsten, editor/*March 1986*
ISBN cloth 0-88132-038-2
126 pp.

WORKS IN PROGRESS

The US - Japan Economic Relationship
C. Fred Bergsten, Marcus Noland, and Takatoshi Ito

China's Entry to the World Economy
Richard N. Cooper

Liberalizing Financial Services
Wendy Dobson and Pierre Jacquet

Economic Sanctions After the Cold War
Kimberly Ann Elliott, Gary C. Hufbauer and Jeffrey J. Schott

Trade and Labor Standards
Kimberly Ann Elliott and Richard Freeman

Forecasting Financial Crises: Early Warning Signs for Emerging Markets
Morris Goldstein and Carmen Reinhart

Prospects for Western Hemisphere Free Trade
Gary Clyde Hufbauer and Jeffrey J. Schott

Trade Practices Laid Bare
Donald Keesing

The Future of U.S. Foreign Aid
Carol Lancaster

The Economics of Korean Unification
Marcus Noland

Foreign Direct Investment in Developing Countries
Theodore Moran

Globalization, the NAIRU, and Monetary Policy
Adam Posen

The Case for Trade: A Modern Reconsideration
J. David Richardson

Measuring the Cost of Protection in China
Zhang Shuguang, Zhang Yansheng, and Wan Zhongxin

Real Exchange Rates for the Year 2000
Simon Wren-Lewis and Rebecca Driver

Canadian customers **RENOUF BOOKSTORE**
can order from 5369 Canotek Road, Unit 1, Ottawa, Ontario K1J 9J3, Canada
the Institute or from: Telephone: (613) 745-2665   Fax: (613) 745-7660

Visit our website at: http://www.iie.com   **E-mail address: orders@iie.com**